C0-DBO-866

Guide to Social Science Resources in Women's Studies

Guide to Social Science Resources in Women's Studies

Elizabeth H. Oakes and Kathleen E. Sheldon

Under the auspices of the Women's Studies Program
University of California, Los Angeles

Margaret Strobel
Interim Director

Clio Books

Santa Barbara, California
Oxford, England

A B C - CLIO INC

Library of Congress Cataloging in Publication Data

Oakes, Elizabeth H   1951–
    Guide to social science resources in women's studies.

    Includes indexes.
    1. Women's studies—Bibliography.   2. Social science
literature.   I. Sheldon, Kathleen E., 1952–   joint
author.   II. Title.
Z7961.023   [HQ1180]   016.30141'2   78-13625
ISBN 0-87436-285-7

American Bibliographical Center—Clio Press
2040 Alameda Padre Serra, Box 4397
Santa Barbara, California 93103

Clio Press, Ltd.
Woodside House, Hinsey Hill
Oxford, OX1 5BE, England

Manufactured in the United States of America

To M.S.
EHO

To S.T.
KES

Table of Contents

Acknowledgments

There are several people to whom we are indebted for their assistance in preparation of the *Guide*. First and foremost we wish to express our deepest appreciation to our professor, advisor, and friend, Dr. Margaret Strobel, for her helpful criticism and support in this and our other academic endeavors. We want to extend thanks to the staff of the UCLA University Research Library, particularly the reference librarians, who were most helpful with our extensive interlibrary loan requests. We would like to thank Louise Noodelman of the Graduate Division for allocating funds for our research, and Dr. Kathryn Sklar, Dr. Fadwa El Guindi, and Dr. Anne Peplau for their valuable criticism of the manuscript. We are grateful to Christine Grella for typing most of the manuscript; to Constance Coiner for typing and editing the manuscript; to Carolyn Williams for research assistance and preparation of the author and subject indexes; and to Toni Daniels and the Women's Resource Center for assistance in typing the manuscript. We are thankful to everyone for their helpful comments throughout the project.

Introduction

The *Guide* originated with the realization that professors of introductory interdisciplinary women's studies courses and those who wish to include material on women in other courses and in their research have had no easy access to succinct evaluation of the social science literature on women. This problem has been particularly acute with respect to material outside the individual's own field of study. The existing bibliographies on women generally concentrate on specific subject areas or are not annotated; though useful, they do not provide evaluations of the wide range of social scientific literature on women. In preparing the bibliography, we decided that book length studies and collections of articles in journals and books would prove more useful to teachers than a necessarily partial and selective listing of journal articles. Furthermore, we have chosen sources that are frequently mentioned in the literature on women or have been recently published. Finally, we were interested particularly in material with an interdisciplinary and international focus.

Organized according to academic discipline and with appropriate subdivisions, the *Guide* includes books, bibliographies, and other resources to assist in research and in the organization of courses on women. Sources were included in particular sections on the basis of their principal theoretical framework or topical emphasis. The annotations describe the contents and thesis of the resource and criticially evaluate it in terms of its use as an undergraduate text. To facilitate use of the *Guide*, author and subject indexes are provided. As graduate students in anthropology (EHO) and history (KES), we were understandably more familiar with the material in those disciplines and hope other areas have not been slighted.

Anthropology

Introduction

In this section, sources on women from an anthropological perspective are presented. Books, journals, and some particularly informative ethnographic biographies on women in Africa, Asia, the Pacific, the Middle East and Mediterranean, Central and South America, and the Caribbean are included. Many of the sources are descriptive ethnographies that highlight women's daily activities or life cycles. Other books present data in distinct theoretical frameworks such as cultural ecology or structural functionalism. Some books explore approaches to the study of women that seek to incorporate a feminist perspective in an analysis of culture and society. Many resources focus on specific issues involved in the study of women: power and authority, status, biological and cultural origins of sex roles, the definition of sexual inequality, and the effect of children on women's mobility. Most of the works contained in this section stress either the complementarity of male/female roles or the asymmetry between men and women.

In the last decade increasing significance has been attached to women's social-cultural roles with the subsequent generation of new data. This data has necessitated a qualitative revision of traditional theory on both sex roles and the dynamics of cultural institutions such as the household.

The reader is advised to consult the History, International sections for additional resources on women of various cultures. The abbreviation HRAF, used in this section, refers to the Human Relations Area Files.

General

1   *American Ethnologist* 2, no. 4 (November 1975). "Sex Roles in Cross-Cultural Perspective."
Ten excellent articles, on women and modernization (L. Bossen), sex differences (P. Draper), women in the Sudan (R. Hays), men, women, and work among the Machiguenga (O. Johnson, A. Johnson), women and symbols in Libya (J. Mason), Inuit women (A. McElroy), puberty rites (S. Parker), Mayan midwifery (L. Paul, B. Paul), female power (S. Rogers), and sex roles in an Indian town (S. Seymour). Good collection.

2   Ardener, Shirley, ed. *Perceiving Women*. New York: John Wiley and Sons, 1975. 167 p., pb.
Six articles and an introduction on women's perceptions of themselves and ways in which anthropologists should view women in culture. Articles include analyses of nuns in a convent (D. Williams), gypsies (J. Okley), diplomatic wives (H. Callan), and Igbo women in war of 1929 (C. Ifeka-Moller). Also contains "Sexual Insult and Female Militancy" by S. Ardener and "Belief and the Problem of Women" by E. Ardener. Articles analyze structure and symbolic expressions of these groups of women and present models of women's roles in each group. Thorough and scientific. Significant contribution to study of women and symbolic anthropology.

3   Borun, Minda. *Women's Liberation: An Anthropological View*. Pittsburgh: Know, Inc., 1971. 61 p., pb.
A brief summary of biological, psychological, and anthropological views of sex differences. Emphasizes importance of women in hunting/gathering, agricultural, pastoral, and industrial societies. Lends support to belief that male dominance stems from biologically based aggression and physical strength. However, sees cultural phenomena as crucial to determination of male/female roles. Provides evidence that challenges view of childcare as constraint on women.

4   Boserup, Ester. *Woman's Role in Economic Development*. New York: St. Martin's Press, 1970. 223 p., pb.
An attempt at global analysis of women in changing economies. Analyzes economic role of women in villages (male/female farming systems, polygyny, colonialism, and wage labor) and towns (markets, factory, professions), and their role in transitions from village to town (unemployment, job opportunities, and education). Analysis based on 1950s to 1960s censuses, surveys, and other government statistics. Presents many insufficiently substantiated explanations of social phenomena surrounding women's labor; however, provides many valuable surveys, descriptions, and hypotheses. Thesis is that modernization "deprives" women of productive functions, and widens the productivity gap between men and women.

5   *California Anthropologist* 6, no. 1 (Spring 1976).
Six articles by faculty members and students of California State University on sex roles. Three essays on primate sex roles; one article each on Quechua men and women, Italian immigrant women, and sex roles generally. Good collection.

6   Clignet, Remi. *Many Wives, Many Powers*. Evanston: Northwestern University Press, 1970. 333 p.
A detailed sociological comparison of monogamy and polygyny in two Ivory Coast cultures. Presents thorough analysis of social, economic, and political

aspects of polygyny. Analyzes type of descent, domestic role of women, economic independence of women, relationship of polygyny to social stratification, and urbanization as factors determining domestic authority in polygynous households. Investigates relationship between women and co-wives, husbands, natal households, and children. Concludes that "cultural contrasts override differences due to marriage types, and that the meaning and manifestations of polygyny vary with the cultural context in which it takes place" (p. 187). Work constitutes major theoretical contribution to study of domestic power and authority, polygyny, and women's roles.

7   *Critique of Anthropology* 3, nos. 9, 10 (1977). "Women's Issue." 168 p.
Seven articles and two book reviews from a Marxist feminist perspective. R. Reiter outlines problems in and new approaches to study of women. P. Aaby discusses Engels's perspective, concluding that complementarity (instead of equality/inequality) and socioecological demands of society should be emphasized in the study of women. J. Moore presents much evidence of the exploitation of women in hunting/gathering societies. F. Edholm et al. carefully delineate critical aspects of reproduction, gender, and sexual division of labor. A. Whitehead and E. Croll review J. Goody's *Production and Reproduction* and D. Davin's *Woman-Work* respectively. Articles make many important theoretical contributions to anthropological analysis of women.

8   Evans-Pritchard, E. E. *The Position of Women in Primitive Societies and Other Essays in Social Anthropology.* London: Faber and Faber, 1965. 260 p.
Contains one essay (1955) that specifically discusses women. Polygyny, absence of romantic love, sex segregation, and low female status, as characteristics of "primitive" societies, are contrasted to the high status of modern British women. Concludes that harmony is best achieved when man has authority over woman and when she does not challenge his authority.

9   Friedl, Ernestine. *Women and Men: An Anthropologist's View.* New York: Holt, Rinehart and Winston, 1975. 141 p., pb.
Detailed cultural-ecological examination of male/female roles in hunting/gathering and horticultural societies. Proposes that control of extradomestic distribution of goods and services is critical to understanding power relationships between the sexes. States that men have greater access to the extradomestic domain than women. Further posits that childcare and family size should be viewed as "conforming to women's work requirements" and not vice versa (p. 60). Analytical depth and scope of this book qualify it as a major contribution.

10   Gallichan, Walter. *Women under Polygamy.* London: Holden and Hardingham, 1914. 332 p.
A nonscientific attempt to present the representative features of a polygynous household. Gallichan draws on historical records, personal communications,

travelers' reports. Data from India, Burma, Turkey, Egypt, Japan, Afghanistan, China, Morocco, and American Mormons. Limited use; outdated.

11   Giele, Janet, and Audrey Smock, eds. *Women: Roles and Status in Eight Countries*. New York: John Wiley and Sons, 1977. 423 p.
An analysis of women's status in Egypt (N. Youssef), Bangladesh (A. Smock), Mexico (M. Elmendorf), Ghana (A. Smock), Japan (O. Pharr), France (O. Silver), U.S. (J. Giele), and Poland (M. Sokolowska). Giele presents important theoretical considerations for determination of status: "political expression, work and mobility, family, education, health and sexual control, cultural expression" (p. 45). Essays address most of these issues. Theoretical definitions, descriptions, and analyses are perceptive and thorough. Important contribution.

12   Golde, Peggy, ed. *Women in the Field*. Chicago: Aldine, 1970. 337 p., pb.
Articles by twelve female anthropologists about their personal experiences in the field. Emphases are personal and academic problems, methodology, culture shock, and difficulties and advantages of being women. Essays by M. Mead, J. Briggs, L. Nader, H. Codere, G. Marshall, A. Fischer, C. DuBois, R. Landes, and E. Friedl. Accounts are highly informative and insightful.

13   Hammond, Dorothy, and Alta Jablow. *Women in Cultures of the World*. Reading, Mass.: Cummings, 1976. 136 p., pb.
A study of matriarchy, women and the family, economics, women's associations, religion, and political institutions from an anthropological perspective. Draws on cross-cultural evidence in attempt to establish "universals" of women's roles. Discusses childcare, contraception, mother-infant bond, marriage, place of residence, and domestic authority. Also analyzes sexual division of labor and women's property. Emphasis is on women's domestic versus public roles, and the political and religious roles of men. While in-depth analysis is lacking, clear and readable examination of women cross-culturally is present.

14   Hammond, Dorothy, and Alta Jablow. *Women: Their Economic Role in Traditional Societies*. Addison-Wesley Module in Anthropology, no. 35. Reading, Mass.: Addison-Wesley, 1973.
An examination of the components of women's roles, including women's work (crafts, household work, trade, food preparation), occupations in changing societies, economic aspects of marriage, and women's property. Draws on data from hunting/gathering, pastoral, horticultural, agricultural, and industrial societies. States that "the data preclude the notion of biologically determined incapacities for any sort of work" for women and that women's work is universally less prestigious than men's (p. 26). Valuable in overall view.

15 Iglitzen, Lynne B., and Ruth Ross, eds. *Women in the World: A Comparative Study.* Santa Barbara: ABC-Clio, 1976. 427 p., pb.
A variety of articles from North America, Europe, Africa, Asia, and Latin America. The first section deals with concepts involved in cross-cultural studies: patriarchy, modernization, feminism. Each article emphasizes "politics" and general overviews of each country, rather than specific topics.

16 Kessler, Evelyn. *Women: An Anthropological View.* New York: Holt, Rinehart and Winston, 1976. 249 p.
An overview of anthropological contributions to women's studies. First section discusses archaeological findings, technoenvironments, political and social organizations, and rituals. Includes observations about cross-cultural characteristics of women's roles. States that "freed from biological imperatives [childcare], young men could roam from home"; "horizons of women [are] thus more limited" (p. 15). Second section presents descriptions of peasant and modernized women. Lacks thorough analysis and incorporation of present theory on women.

17 Lancaster, Jane. *Primate Behavior and the Emergence of Human Culture.* New York: Holt, Rinehart and Winston, 1975. 97 p., pb.
A summary of primate behavior that emphasizes significance of females. Discusses five basic "axes" of social organizations: "dominance, mother-infant bond, matrifocal subunit, sexual bond between males and females, the separation of roles between adults and young and the separation of roles by sex" (p. 13). Also analyzes language and primate communication, and social traditions such as play, toolmaking and use. Lancaster discusses at length important, previously neglected areas: the mother-infant bond (relative to dominance hierarchy); the lack of significant differentiation in food-getting between males and females; the importance of females in decision-making, remembering genealogies, and determining dominance hierarchy of group. Emphasizes importance of habitat in social organization and describes variations between primates. Readable. Incorporates female perspective. Useful in undergraduate courses.

18 Martin, M. Kay, and Barbara Voorhies. *Female of the Species.* New York: Columbia University Press, 1975. 409 p., pb.
An analysis of sex roles, their evolution and differences. Theoretical framework emphasizes technoenvironmental factors and the interplay of biological and social factors. Section one examines data on biological sex differences, primate behavior, and the development of cultural sexual identity. Second half examines women in foraging, horticultural, agricultural, pastoral, and industrial societies. Thesis is that "nature of human sex roles has an adaptive advantage for society, and that these adaptations correlate with group

ecology" (p. 12). Presents many new theoretical considerations and provides detailed descriptions and analyses. Basic book.

19 Matthiasson, Carolyn, ed. *Many Sisters: Women in Cross-Cultural Perspective.* New York: Free Press, 1974. 439 p.
A cross-cultural examination of women's roles. Societies are designated "manipulative," where women feel they are inferior, "complementary," where women are neither inferior nor superior, and "ascendent," where being female is advantageous (p. xviii). Societies discussed by anthropologists are Canada (Eskimo), J. Briggs; Guatemala, E. Maynard; India, D. Jacobson; China, A. Wong; Middle East, L. Sweet; Onondaga, C. Richards; Udu, A. Smedley; and Cambodia (Khmer village women), M. Ebihara. Abundance of useful ethnographic description of women's roles.

20 Mead, Margaret. *Blackberry Winter.* New York: William Morrow, 1972. 297 p., pb.
Mead's autobiography. Includes many insights into her personal field experiences and life as a female anthropologist.

21 Mead, Margaret. *Male and Female.* New York: Dell, 1949. 425 p., pb.
An exploration of behavioral, biological, and cross-cultural sex differences. Attempts to isolate the biological and cultural factors. Draws primarily on evidence from South Seas and U.S. (1949). Theses are that there are biological differences between the sexes upon which cultures base sex role differences; whereas sex roles exhibit much cross-cultural variation, there are some natural behavioral proclivities of each sex. Mead suggests that cultures have not sufficiently developed the great potential of each sex.

22 Minturn, Leigh. *Mothers of Six Cultures: Antecedents of Child Rearing.* New York: John Wiley and Sons, 1964. 281 p.
A cross-cultural examination of effects of "maternal child training practices" on children's behavior taken from HRAF and interviews with mothers in Philippines, Mexico, India, Africa, U.S., and Okinawa (p. 281). Analyzes maternal warmth and instability, time spent with children, responsibility training, and mother-directed and peer-directed aggression training. Concludes that mothers spend less time with their children when other women are nearby to aid in childcare; children are punished more when in cramped housing; working mothers tend to be less permissive than nonworking mothers. Scientific and thorough. Very specific data.

23 Patai, Raphael, ed. *Women in the Modern World.* Toronto: Free Press, 1967. 489 p.
Overviews of women's position in various countries by female residents or natives of each country. Briefly discusses education, political-legal status,

family, marriage, sexual mores, organizations, occupations of women in Burma, Indonesia, USSR, mainland China, U.S., U.K., Scandinavia, sub-Saharan Africa, Greece, Italy, Spain, France, West Germany, Israel, Japan, Iran, Turkey, India, Pakistan, Brazil, and the Arab world. Authors attempt to assess women's status in terms of progress made toward political, economic, and social equality with men. General thesis is that "traditional" non-Western societies are more oppressive than modernized Western societies: "all women who fight for emancipation fight for modernization and Westernization" (p. 17). Purdah, polygyny, and veiling are seen as oppressive. Some valuable information, although perspective is limited, and overviews brief.

24 Powdermaker, Hortense. *Stranger and Friend: The Way of an Anthropologist.* New York: W. W. Norton, 1966. 306 p., pb.
A detailed personal account of author's experiences in the field and in anthropology. Discusses her life as union organizer, student of Malinowski and Radcliffe-Brown, and fieldworker with Lesu in New Zealand, blacks in Mississippi, movie stars in Hollywood, and Africans and Europeans in Zambia. Intensely personal and instructive.

25 Raphael, Dana, ed. *Being Female: Reproduction, Power and Change.* The Hague: Mouton, 1975. 268 p.
Articles that scientifically analyze women and reproduction, power and authority, and social change. Section one consists of studies on sex differences among primates, the influence of hormones on behavior, birth rituals, pregnancy, marriage, matrilocality, and motherhood. Section two includes theoretical articles on women and power (definitions, models, and frameworks for study). Section three discusses female liberation cross-culturally and women's changing familial and social roles in India, U.S., and Africa. An important work. Major contribution to theory development.

26 Reed, Evelyn. *Woman's Evolution.* New York: Pathfinder Press, 1975. 469 p., pb.
An exposition on the prior existence of matriarchy ("maternal clan system"), in which there was sexual equality with a concomitant "nonsexual economic union of sisters and brothers in a horde governed by the mothers" (p. 74). This evolved into patriarchy and sexual inequality. The importance of both early woman's productive and procreative functions and the matriclan declined with the emergence of conflict between avunculate and father, paternity, and the family. Reed asserts that women, through "nurturing instincts," developed "social collaboration" necessary for the group's survival (p. 429). Reed draws on Bachofen, Morgan, Tylor, and animal studies. While her arguments are insufficiently substantiated, she discusses many significant androcentric biases in anthropological theory.

27 Reiter, Rayna. *Toward an Anthropology of Women.* New York: Monthly Review Press, 1975. 395 p., pb.
Seventeen articles that discuss new perspectives on roles of women in hunting/gathering societies (S. Slocum, P. Draper), sex differences among primates (L. Leibowitz), Australian aboriginal women (R. Rohrlich-Leavitt), pollution in New Guinea (L. Faithorn), matriarchy (P. Webster), Iroquois women (J. Brown), public and private spheres (R. Reiter), capitalism, women and underdevelopment (A. Rubbo, D. Remy), evolution of sex roles (K. Gough, K. Sacks), and Freud's and Levi-Strauss's views of women (G. Rubin). This work is a major contribution; essential in the study of women.

28 Rohrlich-Leavitt, Ruby, ed. *Women Cross-Culturally—Change and Challenge.* The Hague: Mouton, 1975. 620 p.
Thirty-one articles on women in Islam, Latin America, U.S., USSR, China, Israel, and on theoretical issues involved. Topics are women's labor and economic position, changing roles and status, and their resistance to "patriarchal structures." Main argument is that egalitarianism (in decision-making, authority, and value attached to economic contribution) characterizes relationship between the sexes in precapitalist society. With capitalism, patriarchy and oppression of women commence. Also notes that "female status is independent of the male power structure" and that "male supremacy" is not a "universal fact" of all cultures (p. 620). Articles are scholarly, informative, and extremely useful.

29 Rosaldo, Michelle, and Louise Lamphere. *Woman, Culture, and Society.* Stanford: Stanford University Press, 1974. 318 p., pb.
Sixteen articles that propose various theoretical perspectives and issues involved in study of woman. Included are discussions of public/private dichotomy, matrifocality and matriarchy, domestic strategies, status of women, relationship between women and nature, and women's associations. Articles by P. Sanday, M. Rosaldo, K. Sacks, J. Bamberger, M. Wolf, B. O'Laughlin, J. Collier, N. Leis, N. Chodorow, and others. Represents one of first important collections of theoretical essays. Essential.

30 Schlegel, Alice. *Male Dominance and Female Autonomy: Domestic Authority in Matrilineal Societies.* New Haven: HRAF Press, 1972. 206 p.
A cross-cultural examination of male domestic authority in sixty-six matrilineal societies. Societies are classified into five types: 1) strong husband authority, no brother authority; 2) some brother authority, greater husband authority; 3) authority of brother and husband equal; 4) some husband authority, but greater brother authority; 5) strong brother authority, no husband authority. Among important findings: total authority of men over women least in type 3 societies where women "play off brother against husband"; matrilateral cross-cousin marriage occurs most in types 1 and 2; patrilateral cross-cousin marriage occurs most in types 4 and 5. Study based on

HRAF sampling and analysis. Useful contribution to study of matrilineality and domestic authority.

31 Schneider, David, and Kathleen Gough, eds. *Matrilineal Kinship.* Berkeley: University of California Press, 1961. 757 p.
A monumental work analyzing the structural, cultural-ecological (or technoenvironmental), and evolutionary features of matrilineal systems generally and nine systems specifically. In part one Schneider presents the major features of matrilineal systems: matrilineal descent, exogamy of descent groups, and sexual division of functions and authority. In part two nine systems are analyzed, by K. Gough, D. Schneider, G. Futhaner, E. Colson, and D. Aberle. These systems are characterized by similarity in mother's brother's role, husband-brother and brother-sister relationships, and control of descent groups over both men and women. Gough analyzes variation in residence, marriage preference, and patterns of interpersonal kin relations found in matrilineal systems as due largely to the ecology or subsistence, productivity, and the society's political centralization. In part three D. Aberle, through Murdock's Ethnographic Sample, views matriliny as one possibility for particular societies rather than one stage in evolutionary development. Provides clear introductions and summaries.

32 Tiger, Lionel. *Men in Groups.* New York: Vintage, 1969. 274 p., pb.
An analysis of sex roles and division of labor based on concept of instinctive bonding of men, which is derived from the historical practice of male cooperative hunting. Women are "neurologically" less able to "inhibit emotional response" and are more inclined toward maternal behavior (p. 67). Male bonding is directly related to male proclivity for domination of political and economic spheres in society. Tiger's conclusions are largely speculative, with little valid scientific documentation. Book is well written and arguments deceptive.

33 Van Den Berghe, Pierre L. *Age and Sex in Human Societies: A Biosocial Perspective.* Belmont, Calif.: Wadsworth, 1973. 121 p., pb.
An attempt at overview of age and sex differentiation in cross-species and cross-cultural perspective. Thesis is that biological factors (genes, morphology, and physiology) set limits on behavior and that there is a "physiological predisposition of gender roles for some traits," such as aggression in men and nurturance/dependency in women. Presents valuable detailed examination of primate societies. Examines sexual division of labor, sexual inequality, age hierarchies, and the conflict between age and sex hierarchies and dominated individuals. Scholarly; thorough in some areas, although somewhat dated. Lengthy bibliography.

34 van Lawick-Goodall, Jane. *In The Shadow of Man.* Boston: Houghton Mifflin, 1971. 288 p., pb.

A primarily personal account of van Lawick-Goodall's work with chimpanzees on the Gombe Stream Reserve, Tanzania. Much valuable data on chimp behavior, including detailed analyses of male and female activities, relationships between the sexes, mother-infant bond, male dominance, and infant care are presented. Useful in undergraduate courses.

Africa

35 *African Urban Notes,* no. 2 (Spring 1976). "Women in Urban Africa— Part 1." 73 p.
Four articles and a book review (B. Chiñas) on women's work in Adabraka, Accra (S. Sanjek, L. Sanjek), women shopkeepers in Nakuru, Kenya (E. Wachtel), women and the fish trade in Accra (C. Robertson), and women and labor in Nigeria (J. Uyuanga). The data presented and conclusions drawn represent substantive contributions to previously neglected areas of study. Good collection.

36 Anderson, J. N. D. *Family Law in Asia and Africa.* New York: Praeger, 1968. 301 p.
A series of lectures given at School of Oriental and African Studies, London, on marriage and divorce (traditional and modern), social change, property, and inheritance. Africa, India, China, Southeast Asia, Israel, Islamic areas examined. Scholarly and informative.

37 Andreski, Iris. *Old Wives Tales: Life Stories of African Women.* New York: Schocken Books, 1970. 190 p., pb.
Brief life stories of Ibibio women in Nigeria, as told by Andreski, with an introduction and comments. Introduction is ethnography, with comments on what are perceived as unusual, "primitive" practices: twin exposure, clitoridectomy, midwifery. Author supports and attempts to deal with prior existence of matriarchy. The condescending commentary judges the women's appearance and morality. The stories have potential use for researchers.

38 Cohen, Ronald. *Dominance and Defiance: A Study of Marital Instability in an Islamic African Society.* Anthropological Studies, no. 6. Washington, D.C.: American Anthropological Association, 1971. 181 p.
An examination of Kanuri (northern Nigeria) marriage and divorce. Discusses sex roles and ideology, husband-wife interaction, and divorce. Men are delegated role of dominance and authority; women, subordination. However, female resistance ("defiance") is expected, encouraged, and reflected in symbolic ritual. "Insubordination" of women is posited as major reason for divorce. Cohen also emphasizes demographic factors, kin relationships, and polygyny as contributing to high degree of marital instability. Valuable study.

39 Earthy, E. Dora. *Valenge Women: The Social and Economic Life of the Valenge Women of Portuguese East Africa.* 1933. Reprint. London: Frank Cass, 1968. 238 p.
An eclectic description of Valenge women's economic and social roles by a missionary, based on thirteen years' residence with them. Detailed description of kinship system, women as beer brewers and cultivators, puberty rituals, and Valenge material culture. Death and birth rites and religious beliefs are examined. While distorted by ethnocentric value judgments, description constitutes wealth of data. No formal analysis.

40 Elam, Yitzchak. *The Social and Sexual Lives of Hima Women: A Study of Cattle Breeders in Nyabushozi County, Ankole, Uganda.* Manchester: Manchester University Press, 1973. 243 p.
An analysis, based on nineteen months' fieldwork, of women's position in terms of their relation to cattle in Hima cattle-herding culture. Elam explains the exclusion of women from all aspects of cattle herding, breeding, feeding, and milking (the main income and source of food) as the result of the conflict between women's childbearing role and the limited supply of cow milk needed to feed humans and calves. "Both offspring [human and cow] are indispensable to group's survival," but mothers are "chief exemplars of human interest in cow milk" (children are weaned early, dependent on cow milk), and "cannot be trusted" with the care or milking of cattle (p. 52). Elam goes on to demonstrate how this opposition is manifested in social organization and cultural ideology of the Hima. A scholarly, carefully detailed analysis, but study leaves many questions unanswered (e.g., why is it that "women cannot be trusted" given the apparent necessity of both calves and children to community?). Does not really incorporate a "woman's perspective." Useful for discussion and further analysis of topic.

41 Evans-Pritchard, E. E. *Man and Woman among the Azande.* New York: Free Press, 1974. 196 p.
A compilation of ethnographic data on Azande marriage, birth, pregnancy, husband-wife relations, family, adultery and extramarital activity in 1920 and 1962 to 1964. Includes transcribed Azande dialogue on these topics. Lacks formal analysis. Distinct androcentric bias.

42 Kaberry, Phyllis. *Women of the Grassfields: A Study of the Economic Position of Women in Bamenda, British Cameroons.* London: Her Majesty's Stationery Office, 1952. 220 p.
Examines "the role of women within the context of economic life... by comparing women to men and by revealing [their] complementary function" (p. 132). Scientific, in-depth analysis of labor, ecology, exchange, kin, and marriage systems in Bamenda. Women are primary cultivators and distributors of crops (through trade), beer brewers, and palm wine sellers. Women have usufruct rights to land from husbands, mothers, and female friends. Women

own and control crops, but men own land. Men, through wage labor and sale of crops, control most cash income. Though dependent on women for food, men have higher status. A thorough analysis; a classic study. Extremely useful.

43   Leith-Ross, Sylvia. *African Women: A Study of the Ibo of Nigeria.* London: Faber and Faber, 1939. 367 p.
Though in some ways dated, views women as important economically and politically to society. Compares women of rural, urban, and transitional areas in terms of economic activity (trade, agriculture), material culture (houses, clothes), Christianity, daily activities, division of labor, life cycle (marriage, birth, widowhood), women's groups, and Western influence (difference in influence on men and women). Concludes that women must be included in development plans. Descriptive and subjective, with little analysis.

44   Little, Kenneth. *African Women in Towns: An Aspect of Africa's Social Revolution.* Cambridge: Cambridge University Press, 1973. 242 p.
Analyzes changing position of women in urban Africa. Some useful data, but overall framework grounded in sexist and ethnocentric assumptions. Unbalanced analysis: fifteen pages on women's political arena, but one chapter each on prostitutes, "the world of lovers," "courtship and social mobility," and married women, thus defining women primarily by their male companions. Despite its bias, it is one of the few books that summarizes material on urban African women, and does include limited material on women's work.

45   Ntantala, Phyllis. *An African Tragedy: The Black Woman under Apartheid.* Detroit: Agascha Productions, 1976. 137 p.
Five articles, some previously published in South African magazines, by a South African woman presently living in the U.S. Essays passionately describe the struggle of black women on reserves and in towns. The combination of personal narratives and individual case histories with political awareness render an intimate view of apartheid. A unique book. Appropriate for study at the undergraduate level.

46   Oppong, Christine. *Marriage among a Matrilineal Elite: A Family Study of Ghanaian Senior Civil Servants.* Cambridge Studies in Social Anthropology, no. 8. Cambridge: Cambridge University Press, 1974, 187 p.
A classic study of conjugal relations based on fieldwork in Accra from 1967 to 1968 with twelve Akan civil servants' families. Oppong analyzes effect of matrilineal ties and obligations of husbands on conjugal relations and "division of labor, resources and power between husbands and wives" (p. 1). Describes families as open or closed to kin obligations, joint or segregated in sharing of resources and household tasks. Least conflict in joint households and male-dominated households. In study, most women were educated, worked outside home, had domestic help, and while dependent on husband's income for high standard of living, saw necessity of maintaining economic autonomy

in face of husband's matrilineal obligations. Important contribution to study of domestic power relationships. Useful in discussion of conjugal power.

47 Paulme, Denise. *Women of Tropical Africa.* Berkeley: University of California, 1971. 295 p., pb.
Seven articles and a lengthy bibliography on women's roles among the nomadic Fulani (West Africa) and in the Central African Republic, Burundi, Guinea, and Dakar. Articles focus on aspects of women and political participation, colonialism, cultural values, life cycle, and position in pastoral society. Paulme attempts to refute assumption that African women are oppressed and dominated by men with analysis of women's roles in marriage payment, kin systems, polygyny, and rituals. States that male/female roles are complementary and that colonialism is "disadvantageous" to women. Very useful, especially bibliography.

48 Richards, Audrey I. *Chisungu: A Girls' Initiation Ceremony among the Bemba of Northern Rhodesia.* London: Faber and Faber, 1956. 224 p.
A detailed analysis of *chisungu,* the pre-wedding puberty ceremony for girls among the matrilineal Bemba. Richards thoroughly assesses the significant political, economic, symbolic, psychological, and kinship-related components of the *chisungu,* basing her assessment on field observations of 1931 and 1933–1934. Succinctly describes Bemba society and the stages in the *chisungu,* and critically reviews various theoretical approaches to the study of ritual. Sees *chisungu* as an expression of "marriage morality," the subordinate status of the wife to the husband, and the reciprocal obligations of husband and wife (p. 140). Also views *chisungu* as an expression of the "dilemma" of matrilineal societies where men are dominant but descent is traced through women (mothers) (p. 51). Richards analyzes *chisungu* from a historical and feminist perspective, consistently emphasizing the important role of women in Bemba culture. This is a classic work in anthropology. Clearly written; valuable for study at undergraduate level and as a source of data for development of theory.

49 *Rural Africana: Current Research in the Social Sciences,* no. 29 (Winter 1975–1976). "Rural Women: Development or Underdevelopment?" 216 p., pb.
Ten articles and a selected bibliography (J. Murray) on women in East Africa during precolonial, colonial, and postcolonial periods. Women, who constitute the "informal" sector of the labor force, inhabit the "private" sphere, and engage largely in subsistence and market activities, are analyzed by P. Stamp, S. Stichter, E. Wachtel, K. Staudt, M. Perlman, J. O'Barr, B. Storgaard, C. Robertson, G. Kershaw, and A. Wipper. Women's networks and cooperation in entrepreneurial pursuits, discrimination against them in farm extension services, the effects on women of rural and urban ties, and "traditional" and modern influences are examined. Excellent collection.

50   Simons, H. J. *African Women: Their Legal Status in South Africa.* London: C. Hurst, 1968. 299 p.
Scholarly and thorough discussion of African women's rights under traditional and European law and the confusion resulting from the confrontation of these two cultures. Theme is women's position of disadvantage in both systems, though in a legal sense there was possibly some improvement with the advent of the European judicial system. Vast information on specific cases. One section on regional differences, one on marriage systems.

51   Smith, Mary F. *Baba of Karo: A Woman of the Muslim Hausa.* New York: Philosophical Library, 1955. 254 p.
A detailed account of a northern Nigerian Hausa woman's life between 1890 and 1950, transcribed by Smith. Baba presents a clear and thorough description of her childhood, girlhood, and four marriages. Slavery, the British occupation, kin relationships, polygyny, seclusion, child adoption, *bori* cults, and prostitution are described. Valuable source of data on Hausa woman's life.

52   Sudarkasa, Niara (Gloria Marshall). *Where Women Work: A Study of Yoruba Women in the Marketplace and in the Home.* Anthropological Papers, Museum of Anthropology, no. 53. Ann Arbor: University of Michigan, 1973. 176 p., pb.
A publication of author's Ph.D. dissertation (Columbia University, 1964) that is based on fifteen months' fieldwork in 1961. Analyzes in great detail "the effect of trade by women on the structure of and behavior within the kin and residential units" of the women (p. 12). Through examination of Yoruba ethnohistory, markets, female traders and producers, Awe residence, kinship, and Yoruba family organization, author concludes that composition of family, husband-wife relationships, socialization and care of children, and women's participation in kin networks and structures are very much "related" to the "independent wage-earning" (through market trade) status of Yoruba women. Although women provide clothes, education, and food for children, have separate incomes from their farmer husbands, and possess potentially high physical mobility, men still retain authority over women in certain household affairs. Women's economic independence does not insure them equality with or dominance over husbands. Author covers topics, including male activities, in detail. A classic work and a major contribution to study of women's economic roles.

53   Talbot, D. Amaury. *Woman's Mysteries of a Primitive People.* 1915. Reprint. London: Frank Cass, 1968. 252 p.
A nonscientific account of rites, ritual, and belief systems of Ibibio women of Nigeria in 1915. Areas discussed are prenatal ritual, birth, marriage, widowhood, motherhood, witchcraft, and women's secret societies. While patronizing, presents much useful data. Lacks formal analysis.

Asia

54 Bacon, Alice Mabel. *Japanese Girls and Women.* 1890. Reprint. New York: Gordon Press, 1975. 333 p.
A discussion of the life cycle of women of the time, court life and peasant women, Samurai women, urban life, domestic service. Much detail, in the descriptive style of the last century; little analysis. Useful as a source for research.

55 Gupta, Sri Sankar Sen, ed. *Women in Indian Folklore: Linguistic and Religious Study, a Short Survey of Their Social Status and Position.* Calcutta: Indian Publications, 1969. 327 p.
Articles investigating women in a variety of Indian folklore traditions. The editor provides an introduction to each chapter. Some articles are more scholarly and informative than others. Useful to those interested in India or folklore.

56 McCormack, Margaret. *The Hindu Woman.* New York: Columbia University Teacher's College, Bureau of Publication, 1953. 206 p.
An analysis of Hindu women's socialization and life cycle based on interviews with ten Hindu female graduate students. A social-psychological framework emphasizing birth and infancy, childhood training, puberty, betrothal, marriage, motherhood, and the Hindu female personality, characterized as group oriented, submissive, psychologically secure, and noncompetitive. Some interesting ethnographic detail, but on the whole dated and lacking in formal analysis.

57 Pruitt, Ida. *A Daughter of Han: The Autobiography of a Chinese Working Woman.* 1954. Reprint. Stanford: Stanford University Press, 1967. 251 p., pb.
A descriptive narration of Ning Lao T'ai-t'ai's life from 1867 to 1938. Her childhood, marriage, and children's lives are thoroughly recounted. Her constant struggle for survival and the resulting intrafamilial strife are sensitively portrayed. A source of valuable information.

58 Ward, Barbara. *Women in the New Asia.* Paris: UNESCO, 1963. 522 p.
Essays on men's and women's roles and social change by inhabitants of Burma, Laos, India, Vietnam, Pakistan, the Philippines, and other Asian countries. Emphasizes sex roles in family life and society. Much useful ethnographic data.

59 Wolf, Margery. *The House of Lim: A Study of a Chinese Farm Family.* New York: Appleton-Century-Crofts, 1968. 147 p., pb.
Study of an extended Taiwanese family. Written in a personal style and based on Wolf's experiences, account describes women in context of family work, family relations, and neighborhood activity.

60   Wolf, Margery. *Women and the Family in Rural Taiwan.* Stanford: Stanford University Press, 1972. 229 p., pb.
An examination of socialization and life cycle of women in a Taiwanese village. Presents much useful ethnographic data. Lacks formal analysis.

Caribbean

61   Blake, Judith. *Family Structure in Jamaica.* New York: Free Press of Glencoe, 1961. 254 p.
Analyzes the duration of, and attitudes toward, sexual unions to explain the prevalence of consensual (versus legal) unions among lower-class black Jamaicans. Based on interviews with ninety-nine women and fifty-three men, study finds that "the common people of Jamaica are suffering from a disorganized family life, that they are aware of this and disapproving, and that although the situation reduces fertility below what it would be otherwise, a penalty is paid in what it does to childrearing and to the competency and integrity of Jamaicans" (p. 22). Consensual unions are usually by "default," and formal marriage eventually becomes statistical norm (p. 153). The view that consensual union reflects social disorganization detracts from scientific contribution of book.

62   Clarke, Edith. *My Mother Who Fathered Me.* London: George Allen and Unwin, 1957. 215 p.
An analysis of Jamaican household structure, based on two-and-a-half years of fieldwork in three communities. Each community displays different socioeconomic characteristics and household structures. Concludes that household structure (matrifocal, nuclear, extended) is not dependent on "external" conditions such as social class, but on particular ethos and other characteristics of communities. In addition, household structure changes with age of members. Marriage (versus nonlegitimized cohabitation) is a sign of status associated with middle age of men and women. Introduction, which surveys literature on Caribbean, is useful. An important although limited work on Caribbean household structure.

63   Cuthbert, Marlene, ed. *The Role of Women in Caribbean Development.* Barbados: Caribbean Ecumenical Council for Development, 1971. 56 p., pb.
Seven articles by church members on women's role in Caribbean development. With the exception of one, authors recommend the increased participation of women in church activities and closer relationship of church with development projects. Robert Cuthbert points out dangers of development that "increases the dependency of the region on external metropolitan centers" (p. 6). With the exception of this article, pamphlet does not constitute useful analytical or research tool.

64   Gonzalez, Nancie. *Black Carib Household Structure.* Seattle: University of Washington Press, 1969. 163 p.

Based on 1950s research, book explores household composition among black Caribs of Beliz. Distinguishes between family and household (members not necessarily related through kin ties). Proposes that "consanguineal household" is "a coresidential group of people who live under one roof, who eat and sleep together, and cooperate daily . . . and among whom there exist no conjugal pairs" (p. 137). Consanguineal households develop because men participate in "recurrent migratory wage labor with low remuneration." This explanation is based on Gonzalez's observation that "it is an almost impossible task [for women] to live alone with children and still manage to raise them properly" without "addition of cash income from some source." Income is "secured from a man" if possible (pp. 51–52). Though sexual division of labor and some women's activities are discussed, study lacks data from women's perspective.

65   Guy, Henry. *Women in the Caribbean.* Jamaica, 1966. 173 p.

A collection of brief descriptions of middle-class "career women" in the Caribbean. Enumerates achievements and membership in organizations. Limited use.

66   Henry, Frances. "The Status of Women in Caribbean Societies: An Overview of Their Social, Economic and Sexual Roles." *Social and Economic Studies* 24, no. 2 (June 1975). 33 p.

An overview of the literature on Caribbean household structure that emphasizes female roles. Concludes that "women are essentially subordinate, and of secondary importance to men—despite the predominance of the matrifocal [or matricentric] family, and the 'independence' which their often unmarried status and economic undertakings supposedly afford them" (p. 168). Points out that the "theme of the dependent woman and her offspring in constant search of a male" occurs often in the literature. Also delineates "women's strategy" used to "circumvent husband's authority" (p. 178). Discusses male economic dependence on females, economic independence of women, importance of female kin networks, childlending, and strength of mother-children ties. Provides good bibliography. Important attempt at overview of female role in Caribbean.

67   Wilson, Peter. *Crab Antics: The Social Anthropology of English-Speaking Negro Societies in the Caribbean.* New Haven: Yale University Press, 1973. 258 p.

An ethnography of Providencia Island that analyzes men's and women's roles in context of whole society. Presents sex role model that cites "respectability" as characterizing the female domain and "reputation" as characterizing male domain in Caribbean culture. Women emphasize kin networks and the church; they are domestic authority figures. Women's authority stems in part from the female slave's higher status as domestic slave and from her association with white society, including the church. Men value virility, drinking, close friendship ties, all of which run counter to "respectability." "Respectability" derives from white metropolitan centers that dominate Caribbean society. Wilson provides evidence of male "crews," comprised of young men who extend mutual aid and information. Important contributions to study of men's and women's roles in Caribbean. Good bibliography.

Central America and South America

68   Anton, Ferdinand. *Women in Pre-Columbian America.* New York: Abner Schram, 1974. 82 p.
Reconstruction of women's roles in pre-Columbian societies based on archaeological remains. Briefly describes education, pregnancy, marriage, social organization of Aztecs, Maya, and Incas. Also describes clothing, cosmetics, hairstyles, food, cooking, and prostitution in these groups. Contains 112 pages of beautiful photographs of sculpture, jewelry, etc. Valuable archaeological material.

69   Biocca, Ettore. *Yanoama: The Story of a Woman Abducted by Brazilian Indians.* London: George Allen and Unwin, 1969. 330 p.
A narrative (transcribed by Biocca) of a Brazilian woman's capture and her subsequent twenty years with four Indian groups in the Amazon region. Abundance of unanalyzed data on most aspects of Indian culture, including social organization, ritual, and belief. Lacks analysis.

70   Chiñas, Beverly. *The Isthmus Zapotecs: Women's Roles in Cultural Context.* New York: Holt, Rinehart and Winston, 1973. 121 p., pb.
A community study of San Juan Evangelista, Mexico. Women's roles as processors and vendors of tortillas and other prepared foods in local and other markets are analyzed. Men's contribution to household subsistence is less predictable than women's contribution. Strict division of labor based on sex and sexual segregation of other activities exists. Sees male/female roles as complementary, manifesting interdependence and egalitarianism. Proposes model based on public/private domains that are further divided into formalized/nonformalized domains. These can be covert or overt. Zapotec women participate largely in private, nonformalized, covert roles. Male roles are accorded higher prestige than women's roles. Useful data.

71   Elmendorf, Mary. *The Mayan Woman and Change.* Cidoc Cuaderno, no. 81. Cuernavaca: Centro Intercultural de Documentación, 1972. 200 p.
Analysis of women in Mayan village of Chan Kom (previously studied by R. Redfield). Presents detailed description of method of analysis, background, setting, and lives of nine women. Data on women and income, property, work, family, and religion. Finds that women raise animals, sell embroidery, bread,

fruits, and vegetables, run gristmill, and tend stores for income that they control. Women and men each feel the other works harder. Concludes that Chan Kom women are less "alienated" than U.S. women. Much useful description.

72 Elmendorf, Mary. *Nine Mayan Women: A Village Faces Change.* New York: John Wiley and Sons, Halsted Press, 1976. 156 p., pb.
An examination of women and social change in Chan Kom, Mexico, based on research beginning in 1952. Revised edition of work (1972) by Elmendorf. Briefly describes nine women from the village's leading family: their activities, relations with husbands, and personalities. Describes family life, childrearing, economic activities of women in village and effects of change on these areas. Concludes that women have important economic roles, their relations with men are not competitive, and women can be initiators of change. Description is somewhat romantic. Some good ethnographic data.

73 *Journal of Marriage and the Family* 35, no. 2 (May 1973). "Women in Latin America."
Five articles on Latin American women. N. Kinzer, on birthrate, disputes myths of passive female, machismo, and influence of Catholic church. High birthrate, she says, is due to female unemployment and illiteracy. L. Cohen writes about Colombian professional women. E. Chaney says feminism in Latin America lacks potential because relationship between the sexes is devoid of competition, and men and women agree on domains of male/female authority. The last article, by J. Jaquette, is a lengthy documentation of activities of Latin American women in revolutionary movements. Good collection.

74 Landes, Ruth. *The City of Women.* New York: Macmillan, 1947. 248 p.
An anthropologist's personal account of fieldwork in Bahia, Brazil. Primarily discusses her private thoughts and a special friendship. Romantic, with some racist overtones. Little useful ethnographic data.

75 Murphy, Yolanda, and Robert Murphy. *Women of the Forest.* New York: Columbia University Press, 1974. 235 p., pb.
An ethnography of men's and women's roles among the Mundurucú in Brazil. The community exemplifies an ideology of male dominance (evidenced in symbol and myth, hunting by males, and exclusion of women from playing musical instruments and entering men's houses), but a social organization emphasizing female authority (evidenced by women's solidarity, matrilocality, female control of *farinha* production). Female authority is attributed to absence of private property and class, and to men's psychological adaptation to their mothers as women in authority. Mothers dominate male children and hence the men "must continually assert [their] masculinity to keep [their] hard won status." "Male defensiveness against the women is in good part an

expression of castration anxiety" (p. 230). Much good comparison to women in U.S. Book written clearly; good description and analysis; absence of difficult anthropological terminology. Useful at undergraduate level.

76 Nash, June, and Helen Icka Safa, eds. *Sex and Class in Latin America.* New York: Praeger, 1976. 330 p.
An essay by J. Nash written from a Marxist perspective and critical of the role of social science, and fifteen articles on three topics: the family and ideological reinforcement of sexual subordination, women in productive roles, and the political mobilization of women. The selections include discussions of mythology about women, women's work and fertility, class consciousness among Puerto Rican working-class women, sexual hierarchy among the Yanomama, industrialization and women's work in northeast Brazil, household economy and women in the labor force in Bahia, sex and social class, access to tools, women in the Mexican labor force, the struggle for equal rights in Puerto Rico, an overview of political participation in Latin America, a critical review of material on the political activity of Brazilian women, feminism in the Dominican Republic, women in the Chilean coup d'etat, and a study of a female Mapuche leader. Presents new theoretical discussion as well as ongoing research.

77 Pescatello, Ann. *Power and Pawn: The Female in Iberian Families, Societies and Cultures.* Westport, Conn.: Greenwood Press, 1976. 212 p., pb.
An analysis of Iberian women's economic, familial, political, and social roles in Spain, Asia, Portuguese Africa, Amerindia, Brazil, and the Americas. Attempts to determine value attached to women, the degree of male dominance, and women's "real" authority, influence, and power in these societies. Attempts to synthesize sociological, anthropological, historical, and psychological aspects of female role. While book falls short of stated goals, it presents much useful information on Iberian women. Contains excellent bibliography.

78 Pescatello, Ann, ed. *Female and Male in Latin America.* Pittsburgh: University of Pittsburgh Press, 1973. 273 p.
Articles on women in Latin American literature, culture, and history. Nine articles discuss *marianismo*, women in Peruvian and Chilean politics, women in Argentinian history, Cuban women, female role in Colombia, female domestic servants in Peru, and professional women in Buenos Aires. Theoretical perspective emphasizes class versus sex and the independence of Latin American women compared to North American counterparts. Contains thirty page bibliography on Latin American women.

79 *Women in Latin America.* Washington, D.C.: Latin American Documentation, 1975. 59 p.

Articles by women from Peru, Bolivia, Cuba, Mexico, Chile, and Brazil address issue of women's oppression. Much good description of domestic servitude, peasant life, prostitution, and strides made toward equality. Thesis is that exploitation of women is part of capitalist exploitation of Third World. Primarily personal accounts. Some useful information.

Middle East and Mediterranean

80   Abadan, Nermin. *Social Change and Turkish Women.* Ankara: University of Ankara, 1963. 36 p.
Describes changes in lives of Turkish women since founding of the Turkish Republic. Briefly discusses legal reform, education, marriage patterns, occupations, sex mores, "home activities," and social position. Analysis based on observable phenomena (e.g., government statistics) versus data resulting from use of formal methods. Limited use.

81   *Anthropological Quarterly* 40, no. 3 (July 1967). "Appearance and Reality: Status and Roles of Women in Mediterranean Societies."
Six articles on women's roles in Portugal, Greece, Turkey, Lebanon, and Egypt. Discussion of life cycles, political and economic roles, public versus private spheres, and status of women. Articles by L. Sweet, E. Friedl, S. Silverman, B. Aswad, S. Mohsen, and J. Riegelhaupt. Excellent collection. Basic to study.

82   Cornelisen, Ann. *Torregreca: Life, Death, Miracles.* New York: Delta, 1969. 335 p., pb.
A beautifully written description of a mountain town in southern Italy in the 1950s. Included are accounts of many aspects of women's lives: as nuns, as leaders of a riot at the end of World War II, as mothers, and as healers.

83   Cornelisen, Ann. *Women of the Shadows.* Boston: Little, Brown, 1976. 227 p., pb.
Portrayal of five Italian peasant women based on Cornelisen's personal experiences. Presents picture of women struggling under harsh economic conditions and living separate from men. Detailed, sensitive, insightful. Lacks formal analysis.

84   Dearden, Ann. *Arab Women.* Report no. 27. London: Minority Rights Group, 1975. 20 p.
Short reviews of women's status in eighteen Arab countries. Regards Arab traditions such as polygyny, veiling, seclusion, and arranged marriage as obstacles in "emancipation" of women. This is evident in areas of education, labor force, and professions. Value of reviews lies in statistics provided on women's participation in these areas. Points out difficulties and progress of

women in socialist countries. Arab women "have said they want to achieve this status [equality] without loss of their most precious Arab traditions" (p. 20). Concludes that upper-class Arab women are less restricted in their choice of professions than Western women and that economic underdevelopment poses major problems for lower-class women in education, medical care, and employment. Report limited by its brevity.

85 Djebar, Assia. *Women of Islam.* Translated by Jean MacGibbon. London: Andre Deutsch, 1961. 117 p.
A defense, by a Muslim woman, of Muslim women's socioreligious status. Author quotes extensively from the Koran, uses brief historical references, and provides numerous photographs. Perceives the Koranic view of men and women as complementary, not hierarchical; the harem as an expression of a man's protection of and honor toward his wife; the "patriarchal" character of the Muslim family as a "recognition... of a woman's frailty" (pp. 30–31). Useful for its elucidation of a particular, though not unique, viewpoint.

86 Fernea, Elizabeth Warnock. *Guests of the Sheik: An Ethnography of an Iraqi Village.* New York: Doubleday, 1965. 315 p., pb.
Fernea's account of her experiences with Iraqi village women. Presents extremely useful material on women's networks, power strategies, religious rituals, and daily activities. Data highlights strict sex segregation between men and women and differences between middle-class American women and Iraqi village women. Sensitive, perceptive, well written. Useful in introductory course.

87 Fernea, Elizabeth Warnock. *A Street in Marrakech.* New York: Doubleday, 1975. 377 p., pb.
An account of Fernea's experiences living with her family in Marrakech, Morocco. Much good detail on lives of Moroccan women. Discusses sex segregation, relationships between women, and women's rituals. Provides valuable ethnographic data, but lacks formal analysis.

88 Fernea, Elizabeth Warnock, and Basima Qattan Bezirgan, eds. *Middle Eastern Muslim Women Speak.* Austin: University of Texas Press, 1977. 401 p.
Readings on women in the Muslim Middle East. Contributions focus on significant characteristics and diversity of the Muslim female's experience as evidenced in history and daily life and expressed in Muslim doctrine, poetry, songs, and speeches. Includes biographical sketches of influential women in Middle Eastern history and of peasant women in Morocco, Egypt, Lebanon, and Jordan. Editors' suggested thesis is that women and men find "solutions within the context of local practice established between the two contradictory poles of Koranic injunction and family and tribal custom" (p. xx). Good collection. Some valuable ethnographic data.

89   Gordon, David C. *Women of Algeria: An Essay on Change.* Cambridge: Harvard University Press, 1968. 98 p.

An analysis of Algerian women's roles and status: "traditionally," under French colonial rule (1830–1954), during the revolution (1954–1962), and after independence. Gordon draws on numerous social and political writings in describing the "feminine mosaic," the feminist struggle in other Arab Muslim countries, the "progressive yet defensive-apologetic" attitude of Islamic reformists, and the opposition to change in Algerian society (p. 31). Under French colonial rule there developed a "very Westernized elite" and a "mass, which out of reaction to the French [became] hostile and more conservative" in attitudes toward women (p. 35). Gordon analyzes in detail the extensive participation of women in the revolution, the "promises" made for their emancipation, and the postrevolution rejection of these promises as traditional attitudes toward women took hold. The return to traditional attitudes toward women stemmed from women's role as "victims" in the conflict between the revolution's goals of socialism and the goals of those who advocated "restor[ation]" of traditional Algerian culture in response to French colonialism. Book provides detailed and thorough analysis of the many facets of women's political and social roles during these periods. Extremely valuable for study of women and change.

90   Hansen, Henny Harald. *Daughters of Allah: Among Moslem Women in Kurdistan.* Translated from Danish by Reginald Spink. London: George Allen and Unwin, 1960. 190 p.

An early ethnographic description of life in a Kurdish village. Generally personal account emphasizes easily observable aspects of women's daily lives: weddings, work, death of children, rituals, dress. Absence of in-depth description and analysis renders book limited as source of data on women. Emphasis on "positive" features of veiling, seclusion, secondary status, and other aspects of women's lives (p. 184).

91   Hansen, Henny Harald. *The Kurdish Woman's Life.* Denmark: Andelsbogtrykkerietiodense, 1961. 187 p.

A descriptive account of material aspects of Kurdish women's lives. Analysis of female status and life cycles incorporated in discussion of agriculture, housing, tasks, clothing, jewelry, birth, wedding ceremonies, veil types, religious shrines, and marriage. Abundance of good description and photographs.

92   Maher, Vanessa. *Women and Property in Morocco: Their Changing Position to the Process of Social Stratification in the Middle Atlas.* Studies in Social Anthropology, no. 10. Cambridge: Cambridge University Press, 1974. 191 p.

An analysis of "the way in which social structure, and social stratification in particular, is affected by the roles and relationships of women" in the Akhdar region of Morocco (p. 4). Rural and urban working-class men who cannot sell their labor in the market are dependent on women who control kin ties, patron-client relations, "extradomestic channels of economic and social help" (that connect women from different classes), and sources of status and prestige outside the market (p. 222). Men successful in the market view women as threatening. "Elite" men use women's networks to increase their political-economic support. Maher thoroughly analyzes stratification, women's networks, market economy, and ideology surrounding exclusion of women from public decision-making. Major work in analysis of women and class and women's networks.

93 Mernissi, Fatima. *Beyond the Veil: Male-Female Dynamics in a Modern Muslim Society.* Cambridge, Mass.: Schenkman, 1975. 127 p., pb.
A sociopsychological analysis of male/female interaction in Muslim society in general and Morocco specifically. Traces "traditional" view of women through modernization and its effect on women's position in society. Perceives the conflict between Muslim values and socioeconomic change, necessitating women's participation in the labor force, as creating anomie among individuals. Female sexuality is viewed as powerful, active, and "disruptive," and "the whole Muslim social structure can be seen as an attack on, and a defense against, the disruptive power of female sexuality" (p. 14). Heterosexual involvement threatens the Muslim system, which is based on male dominance and male allegiance to Allah. Sex segregation (veiling, seclusion), arranged marriage, authority of mother-in-law, and polygyny act as barriers to heterosexual involvement. Analysis is perceptive, provocative. Good for discussion.

94 Roper, Joyce. *The Women of Nar.* London: Faber and Faber, 1974. 174 p.
Roper's personal account, based on two-year association, of the women and their families in the village of Nar, Turkey. Recounts women's lives sensitively. Scattered data on marriage, kinship, subsistence. Devoid of formal analysis.

95 Tiger, Lionel, and Joseph Shepher. *Women in the Kibbutz.* New York: Harcourt Brace Jovanovich, 1975. 334 p.
A sociological examination of the Kibbutz which concludes that the traditional sexual division of labor (women: childcare and service; men: administration and production) persists within an environment that appears to embrace ideology of cooperation and egalitarianism between the sexes. Authors argue this discrepancy between ideology and practice is due in part to the overriding influence of the female "biogram" that predisposes women to desire childcare. Argument is articulate, cogent, and deceptively scientific.

96 Woodsmall, Ruth. *A Study of the Role of Women in Lebanon, Egypt, Iraq, Jordan and Syria.* Woodstock, Vt.: Elm Tree Press, 1956. 85 p.
An analysis of women and social change, education, health, economics, and

organizations in the countries listed. Data from a twenty-one month study is based on government and U.N. statistics, interviews with government representatives of various relevant agencies, and visits to women's organizations in each country. Goal of study was to learn women's "needs for development." Generally views Westernization (e.g., abolition of veil and absence of sexual segregation of activities) as desirable goals.

97 Woodsmall, Ruth. *Women and the New East.* Washington, D.C.: Middle East Institute, 1960. 350 p.
A study based on two years of research on Muslim women in Turkey, Iran, Pakistan, Afghanistan, Indonesia, and India. Briefly examines education, health, economic, political and legal status of women in those countries. A woman's status is measured by her educational level, political and business participation, and stability of family. Woodsmall states that the "most fundamental movement" is the liberation of Asian and African women from purdah. Lacks in-depth analysis; has ethnocentric overtones.

North America

98 Briggs, Jean. *Never in Anger: Portrait of an Eskimo Family.* Cambridge: Harvard University Press, 1970. 379 p.
An analysis of the "patterns of emotional expression" of Utku Eskimos based on seventeen months of fieldwork from 1963 to 1965. Contains much interesting data on Briggs's relationship, as an adopted daughter, with one family (particularly with its male household head). Valuable insight into problems of female fieldworker. Personal, sensitive.

99 Landes, Ruth. *The Ojibwa Woman.* 1938. Reprint. New York: Columbia University Press, 1969. 245 p.
A detailed account of the life cycle of the Ojibwa woman based on Landes's seven months of fieldwork. Emphasizes psychological aspects of Ojibwa life. Observes that men are trained to be economic providers, and to demonstrate leadership, initiative, and independence. Women are taught to be the "recipients" of male economic and sexual "favors." Much variation exhibited in exercise of male and female roles. Marital instability is characteristic. Good ethnographic data.

100 Lurie, Nancy, ed. *Mountain Wolf Woman, Sister of Crashing Thunder: Autobiography of a Winnebago Indian.* Ann Arbor: University of Michigan Press, 1961. 126 p.
Autobiography of a Winnebago Indian woman (who lived 1860–1960), as transcribed by Lurie. Extremely detailed description of Mountain Wolf Woman as a young girl, her participation in deer hunting and in peyote rituals, and her marriage. Much useful data.

101   Schneider, David, and Raymond Smith. *Class Differences and Sex Roles in American Kinship and Family Structure*. Englewood Cliffs, N.J.: Prentice-Hall, 1973. 100 p.
An analysis of sex roles in U.S. based on fieldwork of Smith and Schneider in U.S. and other cultures. Thesis is that class determines ideal sex-role behavior. It is the "values which stress work, achievement, consumption and individual enterprise" that lead to sex-role differentiation (p. 84). Sex differentiation, in and of itself, is "unnecessary as a means for producing solidarity at any macro-societal level" (compare Durkheim) (p. 82). Sex roles are "an ideology for furthering the interests of a particular class" (p. 84). Middle-class norm emphasizes nuclear family and lower-class norm stresses kinship ties (including fictive kin) over nuclear family. Important information. Complex and primarily theoretical.

102   Spindler, Louise S. *Menomini Women and Culture Change*. American Anthropological Association Memoir, no. 91 (vol. 64, no. 1, pt. 2). Washington, D.C.: American Anthropological Association, 1962. 113 p.
A psychological study of Menomini women and acculturation. Using projective tests, the cultural, social, and personal "dimensions" of women's acculturation are analyzed. Values, attitudes, and perceptions of "native-oriented," "elite-acculturated," "peyote cult," "lower status-acculturated," and "transitional" groups of women are assessed. Concludes that women exhibit less anxiety and tension and retain more Menomini (as opposed to white) values than do men whose "instrumental roles" within alien culture prescribe more "rigid" behavior. Women and men experience acculturation differently. Extremely valuable for study of women and change.

103   Spradley, James, and Brenda Mann. *The Cocktail Waitress: Woman's Work in a Man's World*. New York: John Wiley and Sons, 1975. 148 p., pb.
An ethnography of cocktail waitressing based on Mann's field experience as a waitress in a midwestern bar. Discusses men's roles (manager, bartender, "regular" customers) and women's roles (waitresses and female customers) from waitress's viewpoint. Analyzes status hierarchy and networks in social structure of bar. Views men's and women's roles as reflections of male/female roles in American culture. Ethnosemantic emphasis. Much useful data. Important for its analysis of women in U.S.

104   Terrell, John, and Donna Terrell. *Indian Women of the Western Morning*. New York: Doubleday, 1976. 159 p., pb.
A nonscientific study of Native American women's status, labor, appearance, life cycle, family position, and health. Observations and generalizations drawn from material on numerous Indian tribes. Information supports thesis that in traditional Native American society women were not oppressed or considered inferior; rather, they were highly valued for their economic contribution. Some useful ethnographic data.

105 Washburne, Heluiz Chandler, and Anauta. *Land of the Good Shadows: The Life Story of Anauta, an Eskimo Woman.* New York: John Day, 1940. 329 p.
A descriptive account of Anauta's life, written by Washburne from interviews with Anauta. Washburne, in romantic style, traces Anauta's life on Baffin Island to her employment in a U.S. factory. While ethnographic detail is present, depth of description and analysis are absent. Lack of Anauta's own verbatim description detracts from book's value.

Pacific

106 Brown, Paula, and Georgeda Buchbinder. *Man and Woman in the New Guinea Highlands.* Anthropological Studies, no. 8. Washington, D.C.: American Anthropological Association, 1976. 107 p., pb.
Six articles on the behavior, beliefs, and ideology of men and women in New Guinea Highlands. Topics include fertility and death (G. Buchbinder, R. Rappaport), witchcraft and sexual relations (R. Kelly), Fore women (S. Lindenbaum), sexual and familial roles (M. Meggitt), and Kafe women (L. Faithorn). Good collection.

107 Gale, Fay. *Woman's Role in Aboriginal Society.* Australian Aboriginal Studies, no. 36. Canberra: Australian Institute for Aboriginal Studies, 1970. 48 p., pb.
Seven articles by female anthropologists on women's status in aboriginal society and their role in economics, marriage, and residence arrangements. Includes theoretical article on use of complementarity, or "two-sex" model for study of women. Challenges evaluation of women as "chattel" and "profane." Evidence points to women's important economic contribution and their high status and esteem in aboriginal society. Important theoretical and ethnographic work.

108 Glasse, R. M., and M. J. Meggitt. *Pigs, Pearlshells and Women: Marriage in the New Guinea Highlands.* Englewood Cliffs, N.J.: Prentice-Hall, 1969. 246 p., pb.
Ten articles on betrothal, marriage, and divorce in the New Guinea Highlands. Includes important information on sex roles, menstrual pollution, men's and women's houses, exchange of women, and division of labor. Also material on Highland's agriculture and the importance of pigs. Much good data.

109 Goodale, Jane. *Tiwi Wives: A Study of the Women of Melville Island, North Australia.* Seattle: University of Washington Press, 1971. 339 p., pb.
A socioanthropological examination of Tiwi culture from the female perspective. Thoroughly analyzes complex social organization in which matrilineal descent, matrilineal marriage rules, and patrilineal inheritance rules exist. Division of hunting is based on sex: men hunt air and sea animals; women hunt land animals. Important study.

110   Heuer, Berys. *Maori Women.* Wellington: A. H. and A. W. Reed, 1972. 56 p.
An attempt at reconstruction of woman's role in traditional Maori "family and tribal life" between 1769 and 1840. Data from accounts of explorers and missionaries. Largely descriptive of cultural ideology, marriage, reproduction, women and ritual, warfare, and property. Lacks scientific analysis.

111   Kaberry, Phyllis. *Aboriginal Woman: Sacred and Profane.* New York: Humanities Press, 1939. 294 p.
A classic work on women's roles in aboriginal society. Analyzes economic, marital, and spiritual roles of women. Thoroughly documents women's secret societies and ceremonies. Views men's and women's activities as separate and interdependent. Highly descriptive and informative. Valuable source of data.

112   Mead, Margaret. *Coming of Age in Samoa: A Study of Adolescence and Sex in Primitive Society.* 1929. Reprint. New York: Mentor, 1949. 154 p., pb.
Primarily an analysis of female adolescence in Samoa. Theoretical framework is psychological with emphasis on personality, conflict, and sexuality. Presents detailed background of Samoan life, description of life cycle of Samoan women, and case histories of nine Samoan girls. Major finding is that Samoan "adolescence represented no period of crisis or stress, but was instead an orderly development of a set of slowly maturing interests and activities" (p. 107). This contrasts with adolescence in U.S. Much useful data.

113   Mead, Margaret. *Sex and Temperament in Three Primitive Societies.* New York: William Morrow, 1935. 327 p., pb.
A psychological-anthropological analysis of sex roles in the three New Guinea societies, the Arapesh, Mundugumor, and Tchambuli. Based on fieldwork, findings are: among Arapesh, men and women are ideally maternal and nuturant; among Mundugumor, both men and women are ideally aggressive and rivalrous; Tchambuli women are normatively dominant and men are subordinate. While validity of findings is sometimes questionable, study represents one of first challenges in U.S. to universality and immutability of sex roles. A basic book.

114   Simpson, Helen. *The Women of New Zealand.* Wellington: Department of Internal Affairs, 1940. 186 p.
A reconstruction of activities of early British settlers in New Zealand with some account of women's roles. Much detail; little analysis. Little mention of the indigenous inhabitants of New Zealand.

115   Strathern, Marilyn. *Women in Between: Female Roles in a Male World: Mount Hagen, New Guinea.* New York: Seminar Press, 1972. 305 p.
An analysis of "women's roles and aspects of group membership" as contrasted with men's "involvement, loyalties and values" in Mount Hagen. Specifically,

marriage, women's "group affiliations" (with both husband and natal household), and "positive mediatory roles" as providers of pigs in male-controlled *moka* exchange, are examined (p. viii). Though men may perceive women's power as peripheral, women in fact possess a high degree of autonomy through powers of "pollution" in marital disputes and as intermediaries between men. Ideology, marriage, domestic duties, economic role, and legal status of women are thoroughly examined. Extremely important and valuable study.

116   Weiner, Annette. *Women of Value, Men of Renown: New Perspectives in Trobriand Exchange*. Austin: University of Texas Press, 1976. 236 p.
An analysis of Trobriand culture that emphasizes women's roles. Examines men and women in Trobriand exchange, in cosmology, and in the sociopolitical arena. Concludes that women have great sociopolitical importance, which is reflected in cosmology. Challenges Levi-Strauss's view of women as objects of exchange. Reexamines traditional anthropological views of power and authority. Offers new perspective on the topic of power based on analysis of female role. Important theoretical and ethnographic work.

Economics

Introduction

This section on women in the economy includes material from about 1960; earlier sources are listed in the History section. The material is grouped into several subsections. The General category covers sources such as overviews of women in the American economy, collections of articles which include a variety of topics, and one book on women in trade unions. Labor Force Participation includes material on the sexual segregation of occupations and other factors related to women's involvement in the work force. The Development subsection primarily concerns women internationally and their changing participation in developing economies; for further sources consult the Anthropology section. The Occupations subsection lists sources on women in particular jobs, including housework, with the exception of those in the Professional and Managerial Women category. These two occupations have prompted so many studies that they warranted a separate subsection. The final subsection is Working Wives and Mothers, a topic that has a large number of entries as a result of general concern over the social effects of married women and women with children working outside the home. These last two categories have garnered a large proportion of research, while other areas have been neglected. Although there is an increasing amount of historical material on women organizers and women in trade unions, there is little in book form about women currently in organizing and trade unions. There is also a paucity of material on women in part-time and temporary work, on rural women workers, and on women's activities as consumers. The books listed here provide a base for further research on women in the economy.

General

117 Bird, Caroline. *Born Female: The High Cost of Keeping Women Down.* New York: David McKay, 1968. 288 p., pb.
A popularly written discussion of women in the American labor force. Topics include the impact of the Civil Rights Bill of 1964, a brief general history, the sexual division of labor (beginning with the segregation of children's activities), women who make it big in business, the "Negro parallel," new models for sexuality, relationships and careers, and the necessity for sexual equality. The chapter notes consist of twenty annotated pages. Well written and informative, though occasionally superseded by more recent publications.

118 Chapman, Jane Roberts, ed. *Economic Independence for Women: The Foundation for Equal Rights.* Beverly Hills: Sage, 1976. 281 p.
Articles on women in the economy; with the exception of I. Tinker's essay on developing societies, they deal with the U.S. Topics include American public policy, research needs, industrial society, poverty, female-headed households, blue-collar women workers, labor unions, labor force participation, working wives and family income, and credit. An informative and useful book; the thesis is in the title.

119 O'Sullivan, Judith, and Rosemary Gallick. *Workers and Allies: Female Participation in the American Trade Union Movement, 1824–1976.* Washington, D.C.: Smithsonian Institution Press, 1975. 96 p., pb.
The catalog of a traveling exhibition, which includes an essay on women's participation in unionizing activity, a chronology, brief biographies of over one hundred women, and an abundance of illustrations from the exhibit.

120 *Review of Radical Political Economics* 4, no. 3 (July 1972). "The Political Economy of Women." 154 p., pb.
Articles on women's work; the development of economic thought concerning women; women in World War II and war economy; women in the Soviet economy; women's liberation and class struggle in Chile; options of single, pregnant women (with statistical information); academic women and relative deprivation. Includes reviews of books dealing with women and some course outlines. Mostly written without economic terminology; a wide-ranging collection.

121 *Review of Radical Political Economics* 8, no. 1 (Spring 1976).
This special issue on women and the economy includes articles by T. Fee on housework, C. D. Deere on rural women and subsistence production, L. Beneria on Spanish women, B. Weinbaum on women in China, H. Barnett on

the political economy of rape and prostitution, and women and the depression
by R. Milkman and J. Humphries. The articles are informative, but the
economic terminology, which is often difficult to follow, makes the collection
unsuitable for an introductory course.

122   Sipila, Helvi, ed. *Women Workers and Society: International Perspectives.*
Geneva: International Labour Office, 1976. 211 p.
A collection of articles, most of which first appeared in the *International Labour
Review* in 1975. Includes E. Reid on the need for radical change; E. Vogel with
suggestions for the advancement of working women; E. Aventuin on
education, the division of labor, and sexual inequality; R. Dumont on
development and famine; F. Morgenstein on women workers and the courts; S.
Gelber on social security; P. Larogue on widows' pensions; E. Sullerot on
remuneration in the European Economic Community; N. Takahashi on
women's wages in Japan; J. C. Elizaga on fertility and women workers in Latin
America; S. Turchaniova on trends in women's employment in the USSR; A.
G. Leijon on sexual equality in labor in Nordic countries; J. Dhaunija on
handicrafts as a source of employment in developing rural economies; and E.
Krebs on Austrian women and trade unions. Appendix of the texts on women
from the sixtieth ILO session in 1975. Provides a general overview of many
topics.

123   Turner, Marjorie B. *Women and Work.* Los Angeles: University of
California, Institute of Industrial Relations, 1964. 73 p., pb.
This pamphlet begins with a brief historical overview of women as workers.
Topics covered in a general way include the segregation of women into
"women's jobs," laws that affect women, unequal pay scales, women in
professions and management, and unions. Also includes a short statistical
appendix and an eight page annotated bibliography.

124   U.S. Department of Labor. Women's Bureau. Washington, D.C.
This bureau regularly publishes pamphlets and a bulletin that provide
information on a wide variety of topics, including working conditions in
various occupations, wages, hours, career opportunities, childcare, changing
technology, education, minority women, older women, counseling, part-time
employment, unions, laws affecting women, and some international topics.
Periodically they issue a handbook on women workers (most recently in 1975),
containing factual and statistical information. M. L. Bickner has annotated
individual publications in her bibliography *Women at Work.*

125   Wertheimer, Barbara M., and Anne H. Nelson. *Trade Union Women: A
Study of Their Participation in New York City Locals.* New York: Praeger, 1975.
178 p.
A study of union women in general: women in the work force, women's
earnings, women in unions, and the impact of changing social attitudes. Also

discusses women in New York City locals, seven in detail (postal, meat cutters, retail food store, electrical workers, custodial assistants, store workers, hospital and health care, and ILGWU). The authors report the results of a questionnaire given to rank-and-file women on labor union women as rank-and-file leaders. Much statistical information, and specific program suggestions for women in unions. An interesting and informative study.

Labor Force Participation

126   Blaxall, Martha, and Barbara Regan, eds. *Women and the Workplace: The Implications of Occupational Segregation.* Chicago: University of Chicago Press, 1976. 326 p., pb.
Originally published as *Signs,* Spring 1976 supplement, this is the expanded proceedings of a conference in May 1975. Includes M. Griffiths on the costs of such segregation; J. Lipman-Blumen on a "homosocial theory of sex roles" (segregation in social institutions); J. L. Laws on work aspirations; C. Safilios-Rothschild on linkages between occupational and family systems; M.J. Gates on legal aspects of segregation; J. Bernard on historical and structural barriers to desegregation; E. Boulding on familial constraints; G. W. Lapidus on a comparison of American and Soviet patterns; H. Hartmann on capitalism, patriarchy, and job segregation; F. D. Blau and C. L. Jusenius on economic literature on this subject; I. Sawhill on discrimination and poverty among women who head families; M. A. Ferber and H. M. Lowry on women as a reserve army of unemployed; six contributions to a discussion of policy issues; and a summary statement on dimorphics by M. H. Strober. Several papers are followed by discussion comments, and the appendix is an article by M. H. Strober and B. B. Regan on sex differences in economists' fields of specialization. Although some of the articles tend to use terminology, they raise and discuss important issues in a concerned and scholarly way.

127   Davis, Ross. *Women and Work.* London: Hutchinson, 1975. 191 p.
A nonacademic study of discrimination against women in the workplace in England, with some historical background. Describes working conditions, trade unionism, education and professionals, the work situation in wartime, women's attitudes toward work, employer's ideas about women workers, married women workers, and the legal aspects of working. Davis cites the source of sex discrimination as the propensity to deal with women as a group without accounting for individual talents. He provides a great deal of undocumented material.

128   Dodge, Norton T. *Women in the Soviet Economy: Their Role in Economic, Scientific, and Technical Development.* Baltimore: Johns Hopkins Press, 1966. 331 p.
Primarily a statistical compilation, this book provides a wealth of interesting information. Compares Soviet women to American women and Soviet men,

and shows the effect of housework responsibilities on women's contributions to the economy. Also examines demographic factors; participation in the work force; social, economic, and legal factors; education and training; types of occupations (professional and nonprofessional); and achievements in science and technology. Concludes that American women constitute a "large reservoir of female talent" that remains untapped.

129 Edwards, Richard C.; Michael Reich; and David M. Gordon, eds. *Labor Market Segmentation*. Lexington, Mass.: D. C. Heath, 1975. 296 p., pb.
An excellent collection, written and organized from a Marxist perspective, with articles on job structures within industries (steel, automobile), theoretical discussions of stratification, including racial differences, and four articles specifically on women: sex stratification and working women's history by A. Kessler-Harris, women's wages and job segregation by M. Stevenson, segregation by enterprise in clerical jobs by F. D. Blau, and a history of the feminization of the clerical work force by M. Davies. Organized for use as an undergraduate text.

130 Galenson, Marjorie. *Women and Work: An International Comparison*. Ithaca: Cornell University, New York State School of Industrial and Labor Relations, 1973. 120 p., pb.
Discusses Great Britain, Scandinavia, other Western countries, the Soviet Union, and Eastern Europe. Galenson analyzes labor market data: how many women work, at what jobs, earnings as compared with men's, education and training, aspirations, and general attitudes of women toward their jobs. She concludes that women's experiences, though different in some ways, are remarkably similar from country to country in the broad outlines of women's work, and that women themselves can improve their position "if they want to" (p. 114).

131 Katzell, Mildred E., and William L. Byham, eds. *Women in the Work Force*. Confrontation with Change Series. New York: Behavioral Publications, 1972. 76 p.
These proceedings of a 1970 conference sponsored by the Division of Personnel Psychology of the New York State Psychological Association consist of the remarks of participants, including W. S. Heide. Topics include the current status of the employment of women, employment implications of psychological characteristics of men and women, and labor, management, and government policies concerning women in the work force. Comments are brief and general.

132 Klein, Viola. *Women Workers: Working Hours and Services, A Survey in 21 Countries*. Paris: Organization for Economic Cooperation and Development, 1965. 100 p., pb.

After a short introduction on the changing social position of women, their increasing employment, and their family responsibilities, Klein presents material on working hours and time schedules, part-time work, community services, including childcare, the length of the working day for women with families, flexibility of shopping hours, and taxation. She concludes with recommendations for government and employer policy changes, including the increased availability of part-time positions, childcare, and training programs. The surveyed countries include Western Europe and the U.S.

133 Kreps, Juanita. *Sex in the Market Place: American Women at Work.* Baltimore: Johns Hopkins Press, 1971. 117 p.
An important source for material on a variety of topics, including earning differentials, marital status, black women, women heads of families, demand and supply factors (husband's income, education, age), academic women, values of women's work (including housework), future projection, and some laws that will affect women's participation. Primarily useful as a concise literature review and is helpful in outlining information. Includes eight page bibliography.

134 Kreps, Juanita M., ed. *Women and the American Economy: A Look to the 1980's.* Englewood Cliffs, N.J.: Prentice-Hall, 1976. 177 p., pb.
Conference papers from a gathering sponsored by the American Assembly, Columbia University, including W. Chafe on historical background of women's work, K. Taeuber and J. Sweet on family and work, J. Kreps and R. Leaper on home work, market work, and the allocation of time, H. Schrank and J. Riley on work organizations (i.e., not self-employed), K. Moore and I. V. Sawhill on women's employment and family life, P. Wallace on equal opportunity laws, M. Griffiths on legal inequalities and strategy for change (vote), and N. Barrett on future economic trends. Informative; aimed at setting policy, but useful as a general introduction to these topics.

135 Kreps, Juanita, and Robert Clark. *Sex, Age, and Work: The Changing Composition of the Labor Force.* Baltimore: Johns Hopkins Press, 1975. 95 p.
A statistical examination of the changes in work life and the allocation of household time according to divisions by sex and by age. Calls for a restructuring of work schedules to permit flexibility in work hours.

136 Lloyd, Cynthia B., ed. *Sex, Discrimination, and the Division of Labor.* New York: Columbia University Press, 1975. 431 p.
After an introductory essay on the sexual division of labor, articles are arranged topically: female labor force participation, unemployment, and wage differentials; discrimination and occupational segregation; economic aspects of women's nonmarket activities; effect of some government policies on women's economic position; and the economics of women's liberation. An excellent

collection, designed for use by college students. Reflects new directions in economic research on women and avoids excessive economic terminology.

137 Madden, Janice Fanning. *The Economics of Sex Discrimination*. Lexington, Mass.: D. C. Heath, 1973. 140 p.
An economic text that addresses questions concerning the female labor market, the development of economic thought on the "women problem," discrimination and competition, and discrimination and noncompetitive markets. Concluding section compares competitive and noncompetitive models of sex discrimination. An important contribution on this subject.

138 National Manpower Council. *Womanpower*. New York: Columbia University Press, 1957. 371 p.
Study of working women, based on the assumption that "the lives of most women are fundamentally determined by their functions as wives, mothers, and homemakers" (p. 5). Otherwise provides much information on women in the economy (earning wages), employers' attitudes, trends in occupations, the impact of World War II, education, the work experience, sex-typing of jobs, women in the armed services, and work in women's lives. Directed at influencing public policy; now somewhat outdated, though still effective as an introduction to this material. Includes twelve page bibliography.

139 Oppenheimer, Valerie Kincade. *The Female Labor Force in the United States: Demographic and Economic Factors Governing Its Growth and Changing Composition*. Population Monograph, no. 5. Berkeley: University of California, Institute of International Studies, 1970. 197 p., pb.
This important discussion of the changing pattern of female labor force participation covers supply factors affecting female employment, the segregation of male and female labor markets, various female labor markets, and the interaction of demographic and economic factors in the growth of the female labor force. A basic introduction to labor force material. Includes extensive tables and statistical information and a seven page bibliography.

140 Sacks, Michael Paul. *Women's Work in Soviet Russia: Continuity in the Midst of Change*. New York: Praeger, 1976. 221 p.
The focus of this book is the change in women's labor force participation during the Soviet period and the effect of this change on family life. The first part of the book presents historical material from the prerevolutionary and Soviet periods, including matter on women in the nonagrarian labor force. The more recent information emphasizes the time-budgets of urban workers, and work and family in rural areas. The conclusion notes the achievements of Soviet women as well as the continued sexual segregation of work. Although interesting, much of the recent material is in statistical rather than narrative form. A twenty-two page bibliography includes material on theoretical issues concerning study of the family.

141 Smith, Georgina M. *Help Wanted—Female: A Study of Demand and Supply in a Local Job Market for Women.* New Brunswick: Rutgers University, Institute of Management and Labor Relations, 1964. 94 p.
A detailed investigation into the factors involved in the employment of women. Particularly discusses demand, in terms of general employment patterns, hiring and recruiting practices, technological change, wages and salaries, and reductions in employment. The section on supply deals briefly with the general pattern of women's work experience and their motivations. Thorough, though covers only the vicinity of the university and New Brunswick.

142 Tsuchigane, Robert, and Norton Dodge. *Economic Discrimination against Women in the United States.* Lexington, Mass.: D. C. Heath, Lexington Books, 1974. 152 p.
Presents a statistical analysis of women's earnings and employment based on census material and Bureau of Labor Statistics data. Of greater use to researchers than as an introduction to the material.

Development

143 Mickelwait, Donald; Mary Ann Reigelman; and Charles F. Sweet. *Women in Rural Development: A Survey of the Roles of Women in Ghana, Lesotho, Kenya, Nigeria, Bolivia, Paraguay and Peru.* Boulder: Westview Press, 1976. 209 p.
An analysis of women's roles in seven countries based on six to eight weeks of fieldwork; prepared for the Agency for International Development. Conclusions of the study are that 1) women are not incorporated into development projects though they contribute to agricultural production along with men; 2) women contribute to important economic decision-making through their activity in markets and trading. Purpose of project was to determine most efficient way to integrate women into development projects; the sectors investigated include the economy, family care, and community projects. Provides brief, general descriptions of women in these countries.

144 Sethi, Raj Mohim. *Modernization of Working Women in Developing Societies.* New Delhi: National Publishing House, 1976. 168 p.
A discussion of the concept of modernization followed by statistical data on indexes of modernization. Focuses on educated working women; investigates the changing attitudes toward women and education and the changing status of women in a general way. The ten page bibliography is especially good on Indian women.

145 Tinker, Irene. *Women and World Development, with an Annotated Bibliography* (American Association for the Advancement of Science: Seminar on Women and Development). New York: Praeger, 1975. 355 p.

Thirteen articles and an annotated bibliography of 381 sources on women and development. Articles by M. Mead, R. Blumberg, M. Elmendorf, U. Olin, I. Tinker, H. Papanek, N. Youssef, K. Little examine women in Africa, Yucatán, Middle East, and U.S. Also, article by M. Buvinic on theoretical issues in research. Study concerned with absence of female participation in Third World development and makes suggestions for change. Articles are brief but informative. Bibliography very useful.

146 Youssef, Nadia. *Women and Work in Developing Societies.* Population Monograph, no. 15. Berkeley: University of California, Institute of International Studies, 1974. 137 p.
An analysis of the relationship between economic development and female participation in nonagricultural labor in Latin America (Chile, Colombia, Costa Rica, Ecuador, Mexico, and Peru) and the Middle East (Pakistan, Syria, Turkey, Libya, and Morocco). Analysis is based on data provided by official censuses, U.N. Demographic Yearbook, UNESCO Statistical Yearbook, and International Labour Office. Conclusion: in countries at similar stages of economic development, female participation in the nonagricultural work force was greater in Latin America than in the Middle East.

Occupations

147 Benet, Mary Kathleen. *The Secretarial Ghetto.* New York: McGraw-Hill, 1972. 181 p.
Based on nonreferenced interviews and fictional accounts, this nonacademic book is a superficial discussion of the role of secretaries as women workers. Includes a brief history of the feminization of the clerical work force, secretaries' roles as sex objects and substitute wives, and the increasing mechanization and routinization of office work. The constant reference to "girls" is irritating.

148 Garson, Barbara. *All the Livelong Day: The Meaning and Demeaning of Routine Work.* New York: Doubleday, 1975. 221 p.
An investigation of a variety of jobs, many of which are filled by women, including clerical workers, medical technicians, factory workers at Helena Rubenstein, and temporary tuna canners. Garson is explicit in her support for militant unions, her socialism, and her feminist concerns. Describing work rather than individual workers, she interviews several people at each place for a broad view of various occupations.

149 Grissum, Marlene, and Carol Spengler. *Womanpower and Health Care.* Boston: Little, Brown, 1976. 314 p., pb.
This book is about nurses, their work experience, and the process of socialization. Although it contains some useful information, most of the discussion is in the context of popularized psychology involving concepts such

as loving oneself, "saying no," dealing with other women, and path breaking. The issues of occupational sex segregation in health care are cursorily discussed.

150 Howe, Louise Kapp. *Pink Collar Workers: Inside the World of Women's Work.* New York: G. P. Putman's Sons, 1977. 301 p.
An interesting nonacademic book dealing with women who work in occupations mainly filled by women: beautician, salesclerk, waitress, office worker, and homemaker. Includes information on unions or lack thereof, pay scales, and sex discrimination within these job categories. Howe talked at length with many women workers, union organizers and officials; worked briefly in a department store; and attended a homemakers' conference. She includes an appendix of statistics from the Department of Labor, and a variety of factual information is interspersed in the narrative.

151 Lebra, Joyce; Joy Paulson; and Elizabeth Powers, eds. *Women in Changing Japan.* Boulder: Westview Press, 1976. 322 p., pb.
A collection of essays describing Japanese women working in various environments, including rural areas, factories, offices, family businesses, service industries, bars, education, professions, media, politics, and sports. One article on the evolution of the feminine ideal and one on women and suicide. The collection, though informative, is uneven. Some articles are based on research, some on personal experience or interviews; in addition the format of the questionnaires and interviews is not explained.

152 Lopata, Helen Znaniecki. *Occupation: Housewife.* New York: Oxford University Press, 1971. 387 p., pb.
This investigation into women as housewives is based on data from extensive interviews conducted in Chicago suburbs. Discussion focuses on their work activities, attitudes toward their work, the socialization process of becoming and being a housewife and a mother, neighborhood relations, friendships, and community activities. The book suffers from a lack of analysis, as it mainly consists of responses to the interviews and questionnaires.

153 Oakley, Ann. *The Sociology of Housework.* New York: Random House, Pantheon Books, 1974. 242 p., pb.
A sociological study of women's attitudes toward housework, based on interviews with British mothers. Deals with housework as work. The introductory chapter discusses sexism in sociology. The interview topics include what women do, their attitudes toward their work, cleaning chores and mothering chores, husbands' involvement (division of labor), and socialization as housewives. Fascinating, important contribution to the sociology of women and work. Concludes with a discussion of women's liberation and the revolutionary possibilities of housewives.

154 Oakley, Ann. *Woman's Work: The Housewife, Past and Present.* New York: Random House, Vintage Books, 1974. 275 p., pb.
A fine survey of the various aspects of being a housewife, approached from the viewpoint of work. The primary concerns of this companion volume of *The Sociology of Housework* are the historical and political contexts in which women have been assigned the chores of housekeeping. Examines preindustrial and anthropological material which refutes the universality and inevitability of this sexual division of labor. Concludes that the liberation of housewives is dependent upon the demise of the housewife role, the nuclear family as a social structure, and gender roles. Includes four interesting interviews with housewives, which give special insight into the job.

155 Ranade, S. N., and G. P. Sinha. *Women Construction Workers: Reports of Two Surveys.* Bombay: Allied Publishers, 1975. 79 p.
Consists of two exploratory surveys, focusing on changing working conditions through government policy. Information about wage structure, welfare facilities, age when employed, length of employment, indebtedness, marital and family status, and other material on working conditions and living conditions. Detailed presentation on a specific group of Indian working women.

156 Sengupta, Padmini. *Women Workers of India.* London: Asia Publishing House, 1960. 296 p.
Primarily presents material on various occupations in the cotton and jute industries, agriculture, engineering, mining, domestic service, community work, education, cottage industry, health, the arts, law, and others. Also includes information on employment in general, the International Labour Office, trade unions, industrial health, and housing. Thorough and detailed as a descriptive overview.

157 Tepperman, Jean. *Not Servants, Not Machines: Office Workers Speak Out.* Boston: Beacon Press, 1976. 188 p.
Using interviews with office workers and organizers from across the country, this book successfully describes the position of office workers as women workers and as a part of the larger labor movement. The interviews and text also provide practical information on office organizing and how to improve the working situation of women through collective action. Includes lists of relevant printed and organizational resources.

158 Terkel, Studs. *Working.* New York: Avon Books, 1972. 589 p., pb.
These transcripts of interviews with workers (a large number of whom are women in a variety of occupations) about their jobs offer good descriptive insight into American women's perceptions of their jobs and their lives.

159   Wetherby, Terry, ed. *Conversations: Working Women Talk About Doing a "Man's Job."* Millbrae, Calif.: Les Femmes, 1977. 269 p., pb.
Interviews with twenty-two women working in male-dominated fields. Jobs include law school dean, molecular biologist, bank president, butcher, welder, truck driver. The women are introduced and are asked to respond to questions about the requirements of their job, the reactions of their fellow workers (men and women), union activity, involvement in the women's movement. Informative about women's work experiences.

Professional and Managerial Women

160   Astin, Helen S. *The Woman Doctorate in America: Origins, Career, Family.* New York: Russell Sage Foundation, 1969. 196 p.
The thesis of this interesting book, based on an analysis of a national sample of women doctorates, is "that time and expenditures for the professional education of women are not wasted" (p. vii). The detailed information, collected from women who received their Ph.D.'s in 1957–58, includes statistics on employment history, whether or not still employed, career development, obstacles, and family and leisure activity. A final chapter consists of autobiographical sketches.

161   Bernard, Jessie. *Academic Women.* 1966. Reprint. New York: New American Library, Meridian Books, 1974. 321 p., pb.
Based on statistical data, this sociological study of women in academia begins with a brief historical overview. Includes material on women's roles in the university, conflicts with academic men, career patterns, and distribution among departments and subjects. Also includes information on academic women's roles as wives, mothers, or "spinsters." Despite its age, the book is still a valuable introduction to material on academic women.

162   Epstein, Cynthia Fuchs. *Woman's Place: Options and Limits in Professional Careers.* Los Angeles: University of California Press, 1970. 221 p., pb.
After providing a general introduction to women's image and roles in American society, Epstein discusses the socialization process and its consequences, the problems of reconciling the two roles of wife/mother and professional, how the structure of professions affects and limits women's participation, and women in professional activity. A useful introductory text; nine page bibliography.

163   Etzioni, Amitai, ed. *The Semi-Professionals and Their Organization: Teachers, Nurses, Social Workers.* New York: Free Press, 1969. 328 p.
The essays are arranged by occupations and written from theoretical perspectives. Includes a chapter on women and bureaucracy, and a chapter, by W. J. Goode, on the theoretical limits of professionalism. Provides an important and useful framework for studying this job category, which includes

a large number of women. Aspects discussed include the organizations in which they work, attitudes, families, sex differentials, and the concept of professional.

164 Fogarty, Michael P.; A. J. Allen; Isobel Allen; and Patricia Walters. *Women in Top Jobs: Four Studies in Achievement.* London: George Allen and Unwin, 1971. 328 p.
A discussion of women in the senior posts of two large British companies, women directors in general, women in top jobs at the BBC and in the British civil service. The extensive information is the result of questionnaires and interviews and includes individual perceptions as well as statistical informa-tion. Topics discussed include motivation, career patterns, effects of families, attitudes of employers, reasons for lack of success, and salary scales. The conclusion emphasizes need for greater use of part-time workers. Interesting, though too specialized for use as text.

165 Frank, Harold H. *Women in the Organization.* Philadelphia: University of Pennsylvania Press, 1977. 308 p., pb.
A collection of articles and related case studies concerning women in business and the professions. Topics include government policy; sources of inequality, by J. Kreps; statement of purpose of National Organization for Women; sex role research, by A. R. Hochschild; bright women in a double bind, by M. Horner; a rebuttal of the "fear of success" theory, by D. Tresemer; "woman as nigger," by N. Weisstein; assertiveness training, by H. H. Frank; solo women in a professional peer group, by C. S. Wolman and H. H. Frank; academia, publishing, and accounting; and the two-career family (two selections). Designed for use in classroom discussion.

166 Ginzberg, Eli. *Life Styles of Educated Women.* New York: Columbia University Press, 1966. 224 p.
A study based on mailed questionnaires investigating what happened to women who did graduate work at Columbia University after World War II. Discusses the choices they made between home and career, influences in their lives, and attitudes of employers. Limited usefulness as a text.

167 Ginzberg, Eli, and Alice M. Yohalem, eds. *Corporate Lib: Women's Challenge to Management.* Baltimore: Johns Hopkins Press, 1973. 152 p.
A collection of conference papers on women in managerial positions, with a focus on the sociological and economic factors which affect women's employment. Contributors include V. K. Oppenheimer, J. Kreps, W. Goode, E. Janeway, and others. Limited due to conference essay format; a general overview of material.

168 Ginzberg, Eli, and Alice M. Yohalem, eds. *Educated American Women: Self-Portraits.* New York: Columbia University Press, 1966. 198 p.

This collection of autobiographical accounts is organized and introduced by topic: career orientation, family orientation, working mothers, career changes, adjustments in home and work, and dissatisfaction. Useful as a source on women's experiences, particularly in tandem with Ginzberg's *Life Styles of Educated Women.*

169   Gordon, Francine E., and Myra H. Strober, eds. *Bringing Women into Management.* New York: McGraw-Hill, 1975. 168 p.
A collection of articles on various aspects of the work experiences of women in supervisory positions. Includes C. F. Epstein on industrial barriers to women, C. N. Jacklin and E. Maccoby on sex differences, D. Bradford and others on sexuality and executives, C. L. Meachan on the law, M. Strober on strategies, an illustrative case history of a woman being excluded from consideration for promotion, F. E. Gordon on the senior executive's role in recruiting women, and a collection of vignettes of women's experiences. A thoughtful collection, though limited to one section of the work force.

170   Hennig, Margaret, and Anne Jardim. *The Managerial Woman.* New York: Doubleday, Anchor, 1977. 221 p.
Based in part on Hennig's 1970 doctoral dissertation, this book includes extensive information from interviews with "twenty-five women who made it," to document the authors' findings on patterns of behavior and the effect of behavior patterns on career plans of women in management. Their primary conclusion is that men think in terms of the future while most women concentrate on the job they hold presently and thus miss signals concerning advancement; this pattern is explained by examining behavior learned in childhood.

171   Knudsin, Ruth B., ed. *Women and Success: The Anatomy of Achievement.* New York: William Morrow, 1974. 256 p., pb.
These conference proceedings include twelve accounts of personal experiences of successful women and papers on family attitudes and relationships (including a Kenyan example), the impact of education, economic factors, determinants in individual life experiences, and related problems. A scholarly and wide-ranging collection. Originally published in 1973 as *Successful Women in the Sciences.*

172   Lyle, Jerolyn R., and Jane L. Ross. *Women in Industry: Employment Patterns of Women in Corporate America.* Lexington, Mass.: D. C. Heath, Lexington Books, 1973. 164 p.
An economic study of women's employment, with chapters on managerial women and on the role of the federal government in equal employment opportunity. Statistical information and theoretical discussion lead to the conclusion that "the sex-typing of jobs and centrism of firms explains a

significant amount of variance in occupational discrimination among large industrial firms" (p. 51). Annotated twenty page bibliography included.

173 Mattfeld, Jacquelyn A., and Carol G. Van Aken, eds. *Women and the Scientific Professions: The MIT Symposium on American Women in Science and Engineering.* Cambridge: MIT Press, 1965. 250 p.
Papers from a symposium where the participants included J. Bernard, B. Bettelheim, E. Erikson, A. Rossi, and many others discussing such topics as the commitment required of women, barriers to women in academia and to career choice, and the present status of women scientists and engineers. A variety of material and opinions; panel discussions follow essays. Interesting though disjointed due to conference format; also dated.

174 Rossi, Alice S., and Ann Calderwood, eds. *Academic Women on the Move.* New York: Russell Sage Foundation, 1973. 560 p.
Scholarly articles investigate the history and social status of women in academia, research on recruitment and careers, the nature and range of sex discrimination, and remedial efforts. Summary chapter by A. Rossi. Includes information on discrimination statistics, black women, faculty wives, subjects taught, women's studies programs. Presents personal accounts and affirmative action strategies. The many contributors include J. Freeman, J. Huber, H. Astin, and F. Howe. Wide-ranging and useful collection.

175 Spieler, Carolyn, ed. *Women in Medicine—1976.* New York: Josiah Marcy, Jr. Foundation, 1977. 127 p., pb.
Conference proceedings; includes discussion of the impact of women in U.S. medical schools and career patterns of women in medicine. The conference summary provides a concise overview of the topic, and the twelve page bibliography is a useful guide to material.

176 Theodore, Athena, ed. *The Professional Woman.* Cambridge, Mass.: Schenkman, 1971. 769 p.
A collection of over fifty articles arranged by the following topics: the sexual structure of professions, cultural definitions of the female professional, career choice processes, adult socialization and career commitment, career patterns and marriage, the marginal professional, and female professionalism and social change. The authors include C. Epstein, M. Horner, H. Astin, C. Lopate, and many others. An excellent wide-ranging source for material on many aspects of professional women's experiences.

Working Wives and Mothers

177 Barker, Diana Leonard, and Sheila Allen, eds. *Dependence and Exploitation in Work and Marriage.* London: Longman, 1976. 265 p., pb.

A collection of articles focusing on the interrelationship of work and marriage. Topics include women as employees in industry, sexual divisions and the dual labor market, sex and occupational role on Fleet Street, home workers in North London, political economy of domestic labor in capitalist society, the rationalization of housework, the dialectical dynamics of power between husbands and wives, sexual antagonism in Herefordshire, marriage and role division among French upper-middle-class families, and Indian purdah in Britain. An excellent, scholarly collection written from a Marxist perspective; includes a fourteen page bibliography.

178   Cain, Glen C. *Married Women in the Labor Force: An Economic Analysis.* Chicago: University of Chicago Press, 1966. 159 p.
Based on quantitative data, Cain attempts to explain market work by married women, particularly the increase over time. Somewhat dated, little narrative.

179   Cook, Alice H. *The Working Mother: A Survey of Problems and Programs in Nine Countries.* Ithaca: Cornell University, New York State School of Industrial and Labor Relations, 1975. 71 p.
Cook surveyed Sweden, Israel, East Germany, West Germany, Romania, Austria, Russia, Japan, and Australia in fifteen months. She provides an overview of statistics, motivations, rhythm of work life, occupations, education, pay rates, home and housework, childcare, part-time work, labor market policies, protective legislation, welfare, social insurance, and trade unions. Informative though brief.

180   Curtis, Jean. *Working Mothers.* New York: Doubleday, 1976. 214 p.
This popularly written book is based on over two hundred interviews conducted by the author. Includes a comparison of working and nonworking mothers and discussions of return to work, effects on children, childcare, housework, daily difficulties such as commuting, sexuality, "types" of husbands, and career ambitions. Curtis assumes that mothers want to work outside the home, and her book is geared to relieving anxieties.

181   Fogarty, Michael P.; Rhona Rapoport; and Robert N. Rapoport. *Sex, Career and Family: Including an International Review of Women's Roles.* London: George Allen and Unwin, 1971. 581 p.
A detailed and wide-ranging investigation by sociologists into the participation of women in high-level management: analysis of why so few women are in such positions; international comparison between Eastern Europe and Western countries, based on ideology and practice of incorporating women; the relationship between women's career aspirations and family responsibilities, including a close look at dual-career families; and women's actual job performance, particularly as compared with men's. Their conclusion is that "high level careers for women (notably for married women) can be practicable and desirable from both the family and the economic point of view" (p. 473).

182 Hoffman, Lois Wladis; F. Ivan Nye; et al. *Working Mothers.* San Francisco: Jossey-Bass, 1974. 272 p.
A compilation of research on the effects on families of mothers working outside the home, presented in nontechnical language. Topics include sociocultural context, psychological factors, commitment to work, fertility, childcare, effects on the child, family division of labor, the husband-wife relationship, and effects on the mother. No firm conclusions are drawn, but the rapid changes occurring are acknowledged, with a call for more research.

183 Jephcott, Pearl; Nancy Seear; and John H. Smith. *Married Women Working.* London: George Allen and Unwin, 1962. 208 p.
A case study of one British town and its factory where 50 percent of the town's married women work, mainly part-time. It is limited in application due to the special nature of work patterns in that town. Some of the conclusions: 1) mothers of young children were less likely to work; 2) most worked from a desire for greater income, not economic necessity; 3) childcare was the greatest problem; although 4) children were not neglected physically (no judgment on emotional neglect); and 5) it can be economically advantageous for a company to employ women on a flexible hours part-time basis.

184 Kapur, Promilla. *Marriage and the Working Woman in India.* Delhi: Vikas Publications, 1970. 528 p.
Case studies of the effects of working on the marriage relationships of educated women. The emphasis is on marital adjustment, not work. The main conclusion is that it is not possible to generalize and that people's individual attitudes and personalities are central to an acceptance of married women working. Includes eight page bibliography.

185 Klein, Viola. *Britain's Married Women Workers.* New York: Humanities Press, 1965. 166 p.
A study of working wives, discussing their children, husbands' attitudes, work experience, employers' attitudes, effects of industrialization, and future trends. An important early contribution to this topic.

186 Michel, Andrée, ed. *Family Issues of Employed Women in Europe and America.* Leiden: E. J. Brill, 1971. 166 p.
Articles on husbands as providers; two roles of Russian women (workers and wives/mothers); working women and their families in Paris, Czechoslovakia, Poland, and urban USSR. Topics in America include the effects of children, problems of professionally employed married women, historical changes, and the impact of employment on fertility. Informative articles that refute old assumptions about working women and their families.

187 Myrdal, Alva, and Viola Klein. *Women's Two Roles: Home and Work.* 1956. Reprint. London: Routledge and Kegan Paul, 1968. 213 p., pb.

An important book by sociologists, discussing the employment of married women. Social changes that lead to increased numbers of women working include smaller families and longer life span. Comparisons of working women in Western countries, their motivations, employer's attitudes, effects on children, options, and changes that will result from women working (such as men sharing housework). The authors emphasize women as contributors to the economy, and analyze the changing pattern of that contribution. Eleven page bibliography on working women and their families.

188   Nye, F. Ivan, and Lois Wladis Hoffman, eds. *The Employed Mother in America.* Chicago: Rand McNally, 1963. 406 p.
A topically arranged collection of articles, including discussion of why mothers work, effects on children, husband-wife relationships, adjustment of the mother to work. Authors present a large amount of statistical material from their quantitative research. Somewhat dated, but important as one of the early presentations of this material.

189   Rapoport, Rhona, and Robert N. Rapoport. *Dual-Career Families.* Baltimore: Penguin, 1971. 327 p., pb.
Five case studies from the authors' analytic study with M. Fogarty, *Sex, Career and Family* (no. 181). These interviews investigating how marriages are affected by both men and women working at professional-level jobs emphasize patterns of decision-making and division of labor.

190   Sweet, James A. *Women in the Labor Force.* New York: Seminar Press, 1973. 211 p.
Emphasis is on women, work, and families in this study based on a cross-sectional data base. Introduction includes a review of the literature of "factors influencing the employment of wives." Information on labor force activity of wives in relation to family composition, including the status of children and family histories; family status generally in terms of education, economic need, and labor force activity; the earnings of wives and black-white differences in wives' wages and contribution to family income. Data base is limited to the 1960 U.S. census information on married, nonfarm women under sixty who are living with their husbands. Includes much useful information but little analysis.

191   Yudkin, Simon, and Anthea Holme. *Working Mothers and Their Children.* London: Michael Joseph, 1963. 199 p.
An early discussion of this topic with special emphasis on the effects of mothers' working on fatherless families and on children, including the "problems of substitute care." The authors review the literature on the effects on children and conclude that there is much dogmatism and little evidence concerning working mothers and their children. Generally supportive of the working mother; suggests changes necessary to ease her burdens.

History

Introduction

This section contains a wide variety of historical writings that concern women. The General section consists of classic studies, historiographic selections, and international studies that extend beyond the other subsections. The United States histories have been divided into two categories: General includes both overviews and special studies on topics such as Victorian women, intellectual history, black women, birth control, Southern women, and many others, often with a focus on social change; Suffrage and Women's Movement has material primarily on the nineteenth-century movement, including participant reports and contributions on the ideas and attitudes of these movements. The International/General subsection contains non-European and non-U.S. material on a variety of topics; most contributions are on Third World women's history, although Canada and the Soviet Union are included. The material in the International/Europe subsection encompasses various special topics, ranging from women of antiquity to medieval women to twentieth-century women. Finally, the Economic History subsection contains pre-1960 sources; for more recent information check the Economics section. Most of these contributions are descriptive of women's past economic activities, though analytic studies are also included. This section as a whole includes documentary material, descriptive and analytic contributions, and collections of articles.

General

192   Beard, Mary R. *Woman as Force in History: A Study in Traditions and Realities.* 1946. Reprint. New York: Collier, 1973. 369 p., pb.
A classic in the study of women's history. In large part a discussion of legal history, particularly focusing on Blackstone as an example of the promulgation of oppressive, restrictive attitudes toward women's position. Includes information from ancient and medieval times on the involvement of women in politics, philosophy, and other areas. Disproves widespread popular belief in the historically passive role of women. Extensive, annotated, twenty-five page bibliography.

193   Bebel, August. *Women under Socialism.* Translated by Daniel de Leon. 1883. Reprint. New York: Schocken Books, 1971. 379 p., pb.
A classic Marxist discussion on the condition of women and its relation to the origins of private property. Includes outdated historical and anthropological information, discussion of women and marriage, prostitution, women and work, overpopulation, struggles for equality, and more general discussion of capitalist society and the possibilities of socialism.

194   Boulding, Elise. *The Underside of History: A View of Women through Time.* Boulder: Westview Press, 1976. 829 p.
An impressive, readable attempt to outline world history, with a focus on women, beginning with prehistoric times. The first section presents a succinct summary of anthropological information, "setting the stage" of sexual division of labor. Throughout, Boulding writes about common women as well as famous women. She includes different world areas, although the West is most frequently discussed, particularly the post-1450 period. The primary limitation inherent in such a work is the generalization necessary to cover such vast space and time. Useful as introduction to various areas, although every specialist will feel her area was shortchanged.

195   Boulding, Elise. *Women in the Twentieth Century World.* New York: John Wiley and Sons, Halsted Press, 1977. 264 p.
Material originally prepared in 1975 as lectures on women in the twentieth century. Includes information on historical background, women and productive systems, women and the international system. Specific topics include nomadism and women's status, food systems, world peace, and women's "nongovernmental organizations." Boulding's orientation is international; she has worked with U.N. information and programs.

196   Bullough, Vern L., and Bonnie Bullough. *The Subordinate Sex: A History of Attitudes toward Women.* Urbana: University of Illinois Press, 1973. 375 p.
A thorough study of attitudes toward women beginning in classical times. Includes information on ancient Greece and Rome, early Christianity, Byzantium, Islam, medieval Europe, China, India, and industrialized Europe and America. Twelve page bibliography.

197   Deckard, Barbara. *The Women's Movement: Political, Socioeconomic, and Psychological Issues.* New York: Harper and Row, 1975. 450 p., pb.
A readable, comprehensive discussion of all aspects of women's history and present status. Part one proceeds from a presentation of psychological theories and sex-role socialization to the role of the family, the exploitation of working women, women in professions, and women and the law. Part two covers women's place throughout history, beginning with prehistorical evidence. Discusses the differences between capitalist and socialist societies, including the Third World. Includes material about the struggle in America for suffrage and women's rights, the period of 1920 to 1960, and the trends in the current women's movement. Deckard's style is objective though she does not hide her feminist concerns.

198   Ehrenreich, Barbara, and Deirdre English. *Witches, Midwives and Nurses: A History of Women Healers.* Old Westbury, N.Y.: Feminist Press, 1973. 43 p., pb.

An important history of the suppression of women healers (witches and midwives); surveys the development of the present system of male doctors and female nurses and the results for female patients.

199 Forbes, Thomas Rogers. *The Midwife and the Witch.* New Haven: Yale University Press, 1966. 196 p.
A history of superstition and practice concerning pregnancy and childbirth based on extensive library research. Descriptive, not analytic. Includes information on early licensing of midwives. The thirty-five page bibliography has many Latin, German, and obscure sources.

200 Forfreedom, Ann, ed. *Women Out of History: A Herstory Anthology.* Los Angeles: Ann Forfreedom, 1972. 255 p., pb.
An assortment of writings on feminism and women's history. Assumes the historical existence of matriarchies; much space given to Amazon cultures and women's religion (witches). Includes excerpts from H. Diner, M. Beard, and many others, with connective essays by A. Forfreedom. A personal historical vision; disjointed.

201 Hartman, Mary S., and Lois Banner, ed. *Clio's Consciousness Raised: New Perspectives on the History of Women.* New York: Harper and Row, 1974. 253 p., pb.
Topics of the articles in the collection include women's diseases and their treatment in nineteenth-century America; the cycle of femininity; the "Lady" and her physician; the beginnings of feminist birth control ideas; French women and the professions; sexual politics of Victorian social anthropology; women's power in the medieval European family (500–1100); domestic feminism in Victorian America; feminization of American religion; feminization of public librarianship; the myth of the idle Victorian woman; prostitution and the poor in Plymouth; the welfare of women in English laboring families (1860–1950); and a case study of technology, the washing machine and the working wife. A wide-ranging, scholarly collection. Papers were originally presented at the 1973 Berkshire Conference of Women Historians, and many are also available in *Feminist Studies.*

202 Mill, John Stuart, and Harriet Taylor Mill. *Essays on Sex Equality.* Edited by Alice S. Rossi. Chicago: University of Chicago Press, 1970. 242 p., pb.
This is a collection of all the authors' writings on sex equality: "Early Essays on Marriage and Divorce," "Enfranchisement of Women," and "The Subjection of Women." A. Rossi has contributed a thoughtful essay on the intellectual relationship of J. S. Mill and H. T. Mill.

203 Morewedge, Rosemarie Thee, ed. *The Role of Women in the Middle Ages.* Albany: State University of New York Press, 1975. 195 p.

The topics of these 1972 conference papers include life expectancies, women in literature, Isolt and Guenevere, Petrarch's Laura, the writings of Christine de Pizan on women in medieval society, and women in manuscript margins. Scholarly and informative.

204   O'Neill, William L. *The Woman Movement: Feminism in the United States and England.* New York: Barnes and Noble, 1969. 208 p.
A lengthy historical essay and selected documents on women in public life in the nineteenth and early twentieth centuries. Not restricted to the suffragist movement; information and material on women in other reform movements (abolition, the struggle for improved working conditions) is included, as is discussion of the women's club movement.

205   Rossi, Alice S., ed. *The Feminist Papers: From Adams to de Beauvoir.* New York: Bantam Books, 1973. 716 p., pb.
A comprehensive anthology of major feminist writings, mostly from the American experience. A. Rossi introduces each section, setting the selections in their historical context, and includes introductory comments on the various authors. Contributors from the era of the Enlightenment include A. Adams, M. Wollstonecraft, F. Wright, and M. Fuller; from the 1800s, A. and S. Grimke, E. Blackwell, and E. C. Stanton; on class politics and feminism, F. Engels, A. Bebel, E. Goldman, M. Sanger, C. P. Gilman, and J. Addams; and on "intellectual complexity," V. Woolf, M. Mead, and S. de Beauvoir.

206   Rowbotham, Sheila. *Women, Resistance, and Revolution: A History of Women and Revolution in the Modern World.* New York: Random House, Vintage Books, 1972. 288 p., pb.
The history of women in revolutionary movements in Europe, the U.S., Russia, China, Cuba, Algeria, and Vietnam. Discusses the limits and usefulness of Marx's and Engels's writings on women, and relates the past to the present. An excellent overview and discussion of the connections and contradictions of feminism and socialism.

207   Schneir, Miriam, ed. *Feminism: The Essential Historical Writings.* New York: Random House, 1972. 360 p.
A very useful collection of primarily American selections from 1776 to 1929. Limited to topics of current relevance such as marriage, economic dependence, and "selfhood" (suffrage is excluded). The introductions to each piece provide useful background information. Type of material includes fiction, autobiography, lectures, and letters, many of them classic and often-quoted sources. Schneir has deliberately included selections by and about black and working-class women.

208   Thompson, Roger. *Women in Stuart England and America: A Comparative Study.* London: Routledge and Kegan Paul, 1974. 276 p.

Compares seventeenth-century women of England with those in colonial Massachusetts and Virginia. Thesis is "the relative emancipation of women in the American colonies" (p. 11). Discusses economic opportunity, religion (the Puritan churches), frontier experiences, courtship and marriage, the family, legal position and rights, education, the vote. One chapter analyzes the general attitude or "moral tone" in each area. Scholarly, though much information is from secondary sources.

209 White, Cynthia L. *Women's Magazines 1693–1968.* London: Michael Joseph, 1970. 348 p.
A meticulous study, from the origins of a women's press to the recent proliferation of mass market women's magazines in Great Britain and America. White includes many quotes from the magazines and several appendixes with information on circulation and editorial content. A useful overview; includes a list of women's periodicals (pp. 304–17).

210 *Women and Communism: Selections from the Writings of Marx, Engels, Lenin, and Stalin.* 1950. Reprint. Westport, Conn.: Greenwood Press, 1973. 104 p.
Material is arranged by topic, beginning with the "enslavement" of women and including women under capitalism (their exploitation, the bourgeois family, and the struggle for socialism), and socialism and the emancipation of women.

United States / General

211 Altbach, Edith Hoshino. *Women in America.* Lexington, Mass.: D. C. Heath, 1974. 205 p., pb.
This book is divided into two parts. The first section concerns women and work, both currently and historically, with special emphasis on housework and women in the labor force, including unionization. The second section is on feminist activism and again includes an historical discussion of the earlier women's movement and information on the new feminism, with a case study of the struggle for day care. The attempt to cover a wide range of material sometimes leads to superficiality, but generally Altbach's information is good.

212 Banner, Lois W. *Women in Modern America: A Brief History.* New York: Harcourt Brace Jovanovich, 1974. 276 p., pb.
Banner begins her history of women in 1890; it covers all aspects of women's lives, including medicine, the mass media, the suffrage movement, education, work, women's organizations, prostitution, and the various strands of the present women's movement. Many photographs. Each section is followed by a critical bibliography. Generally a readable and useful book, geared to high school and younger readers.

213   Barker-Benfield, G. J. *The Horrors of the Half-Known Life: Male Attitudes toward Women and Sexuality in Nineteenth-Century America.* New York: Harper and Row, 1976. 352 p., pb.
This history is divided into four sections: an overview of sexual segregation, derived from A. de Tocqueville; an account of the banishment of midwives at the hands of obstetricians, including information on J. Marion Sims and female castration; an analysis of Reverend John Todd's writings for young men (including masturbation phobia and "spermatic economy"); Augustus Kinsley Gardner and obstetrics and gynecology. Focus is primarily psychoanalytical and biographical.

214   Benson, Mary Sumner. *Women in Eighteenth Century America: A Study of Opinion and Social Usage.* New York: Columbia University Press, 1935. 343 p.
An important study of opinions about women. Traces the European origin of American ideas on the status of women and includes material on women in early American literature, law, politics, and the church. Seventeen page bibliographic essay.

215   Brent, Linda (Harriet Brent Jacobs). *Incidents in the Life of A Slave Girl.* Edited by L. Maria Child. 1861. Reprint. New York: Harcourt Brace Jovanovich, 1973. 210 p., pb.
One of the few slave narratives written by a woman; it describes the special abuses to which female slaves were subjected. An historical document that is readily available and readable; speaks of the lot of slave women through the story of L. Brent's own life in slavery, her escape, and her life in the North. The 1973 edition has an introduction and notes by Walter Toller.

216   Brown, Dee. *The Gentle Tamers: Women of the Old Wild West.* New York: G. P. Putnam's Sons, 1958. 317 p., pb.
An anecdotal history of women in the American West. Although racist and sexist regarding Indians ("in his primitive way . . .," p. 28), it does include quotes from diaries, letters, and memoirs that report some of women's experiences.

217   Chafe, William H. *The American Woman: Her Changing Social, Economic, and Political Roles, 1920–1970.* New York: Oxford University Press, 1972. 351 p., pb.
Thorough and sympathetic study of women in this period. Describes political activity, economic status, conditions in industry and the professions, and the beginnings of Equal Rights Amendment legislation. Excellent on World War II and its impact, the 1950s debate on woman's place, and the revival of feminism in the 1960s. Includes twenty page bibliography.

218   Chafe, William H. *Women and Equality: Changing Patterns in American Culture.* New York: Oxford University Press, 1977. 207 p.

A collection of essays on social change, with the position of women as the reference point. After a brief introduction on defining and approaching women's history, Chafe presents an historical overview; two lengthy sections paralleling the cases of racism and sexism in social control and social change; a discussion of 1970s feminism in historical perspective; and a final essay, "Where Do We Go from Here." The emphasis is on the attainment of sexual equality, and the attendant risks and possibilities. A consciousness of class and race differences runs throughout.

219 Conrad, Susan Phinney. *Perish the Thought: Intellectual Women in Romantic America, 1830–1860.* New York: Oxford University Press, 1976. 292 p.
A scholarly study of women intellectuals in pre–Civil War America, their conflicts with ideals of womanhood, and society's restrictions on their activities (such as the absence of universities). Focuses on individuals; useful to those studying this particular aspect of U.S. or women's history.

220 Cotera, Martha. *Diosa y hembra: The History and Heritage of Chicanas in the U.S.* Austin: Information Systems Development, 1976. 202 p., pb.
A detailed social history and commentary on Mexican women in Mexico and the U.S. Also briefly analyzes women and labor, the family, political participation and resistance. Throughout, individual women are cited for particular contributions or achievements—a final section is devoted entirely to these citations. Some observations are that Chicana labor force participation is lower than that of other women in the U.S., and that the "macho/subservient female" stereotype of male/female relationships has no real basis (p. 154). Much useful information. A basic book on the Chicana.

221 Cott, Nancy F. *The Bonds of Womanhood: "Woman's Sphere" in New England, 1780–1835.* New Haven: Yale University Press, 1977. 225 p., pb.
Investigation of bonds between women and bonds that oppress women; covers five subtopics: work, domesticity, education, religion, and sisterhood. Evidence of bonds is diaries, letters, and other written sources by primarily middle- and upper-middle-class white women. The selections offer fascinating glimpses of women's perceptions of their lives and experiences.

222 Cott, Nancy F., ed. *Root of Bitterness: Documents of the Social History of American Women.* New York: E. P. Dutton, 1972. 373 p., pb.
An essay and documents on women's social history from colonial times to 1900. The collection emphasizes women's personal experiences as seen in diaries, letters, and stories. Includes testimony from the Salem witch trials and narratives of escaped slaves. Topics range from revolutionary war and pioneer experiences to nineteenth-century health issues, women in nineteenth-century industry, and women of leisure.

223 Dannett, Sylvia G. L., ed. *Noble Women of the North.* New York: Thomas Yoseloff, 1959. 419 p.
An annotated collection of letters, diaries, and memoirs of women of the North who were active in the abolition movement at the time of the Civil War. Fascinating reading, but most useful for researchers.

224 De Pauw, Linda Grant, and Conover Hunt. *Remember the Ladies: Women in America 1750–1815.* New York: Viking Press, 1976. 168 p.
An exhibition catalog, well illustrated with examples of material culture and arranged by topic: love and marriage, motherhood, sickness and death, domesticity, women at work, women and religion, women at war, accomplished women, fashionable ladies, creative women, presidents' ladies, and liberty and equality. Includes black and Indian women. Interesting and informative, particularly the illustrations of material goods and women's handicrafts.

225 Fischer, Christiane, ed. *Let Them Speak for Themselves: Women in the American West, 1849–1900.* Hamden, Conn.: Archon Books, 1977. 346 p.
Selections from letters, diaries, and memoirs of female pioneers, introduced and annotated by Fischer. Includes material on mining camps and towns, farms and ranches, the army, working women, urban life, childhood, and travelers. Many of these were previously inaccessible, and provide fascinating insight into women's experiences. Twelve page bibliography.

226 Friedman, Jean E., and William G. Shade, ed. *Our American Sisters: Women in American Life and Thought.* Boston: Allyn and Bacon, 1973. 354 p.
Collection of previously published articles on women in American history, colonial times to the present. Includes selections by such historians as E. S. Morgan, J. Demos, J. C. Spruill, W. Jordan, G. Lerner, A. F. Scott, C. Lasch, C. N. Degler, A. S. Kraditor, and W. O'Neill. A comprehensive collection of important, often-quoted articles, covering both the feminist movement and women's social history.

227 George, Carol V. R., ed. *"Remember the Ladies": New Perspectives on Women in American History: Essays in Honor of Nelson Manfred Blake.* Syracuse: Syracuse University Press, 1975. 201 p.
An original, scholarly collection dealing with women and social change. Three sections: religious and ideological influences, 1600 to 1800 (articles on Anne Hutchinson, Abigail Adams and Puritanism, and eighteenth-century theorists of women's liberation); "The Cult of True Womanhood" (articles on Harriet Tubman, "man-midwifery," and the nativist movement); and social change (divorce, flappers, Japanese echoes of American cultural feminism, and the founding of the U.S. Children's Bureau). George introduces each section.

228 Gordon, Ann D.; Mari Jo Buhle; and Nancy Schrom Dye. *Women in American Society: An Historical Contribution.* Somerville, Mass.: New England Free Press, 1972. 64 p., pb.
First published in *Radical America* (July–August 1971), this is an excellent overview of the social history of American women, with a sharp awareness of class differences. The authors conclude that "despite economic, technological, and social change, the ideological assumptions affecting women have remained strikingly familiar" (p. 50). Thirteen pages of annotated footnotes.

229 Gordon, Linda. *Woman's Body, Woman's Right: A Social History of Birth Control in America.* New York: Grossman, 1976. 479 p., pb.
An extensive history of birth control including methods and folklore, changing attitudes toward sexuality, the relationship between the women's movements and birth control movements. All is set in a sound base of the interrelatedness of economics and history as they affect social attitudes and social movements. Thesis is that women have always sought control of reproduction.

230 Hogeland, Ronald W., ed. *Women and Womanhood in America.* Lexington, Mass.: D. C. Heath, 1973. 183 p., pb.
The articles are arranged in pairs so that an "opinion" or "observation" is followed by a "commentary" or "critique." Topics and contributors are A. S. Kraditor and G. Lerner on studying women in American history; C. Mather, T. Jefferson, W. Jordan, A. Stanford, and W. O'Meara on colonial America; A. de Tocqueville, C. Beecher, G. Lerner, B. Welter, and D. Meyer on nineteenth-century women; C. P. Gilman, B. Spock, F. Beal, D. Kennedy, and A. Rossi on the twentieth century. These articles are readily available elsewhere.

231 Janeway, Elizabeth, ed. *Women: Their Changing Roles.* New York: New York Times/Arno Press, 1973. 556 p.
New York Times articles from 1928 to 1972 concerning women, arranged chronologically and by topics: social feminism, women in the arts, sexuality, politics. Fascinating, but is reduced newsprint and so is not easy to read.

232 Kennedy, David M. *Birth Control in America: The Career of Margaret Sanger.* New Haven: Yale University Press, 1970. 320 p., pb.
A history of the birth control movement, 1912 to World War II, with Sanger as the central figure. Provides some historical and social background, though could be more useful for researchers.

233 Lemons, J. Stanley. *The Woman Citizen: Social Feminism in the 1920s.* Urbana: University of Illinois Press, 1973. 266 p.
Considers aspects of feminism and progressivism: "One of my principal contentions is that the social feminists constituted an important link in the

chain from the progressive era to the New Deal" (p. viii). Actually begins with World War I and covers the period through 1933. Interesting chapter on red-baiting attacks on women reformers, but no discussion of socialist women. Detailed and scholarly, particularly concerned with organizations. Ten page bibliographic essay.

234 Lerner, Gerda, ed. *Black Women in White America: A Documentary History.* New York: Random House, Vintage Books, 1972. 630 p., pb.
A fascinating and diverse collection of writings by and about black women from slavery to the present. Includes selections from diaries, letters, autobiographies, court testimonies, and other sources. Topics include slavery, the struggle for education, sex crimes and politics, "Making a Living," "Survival is a Form of Resistance," "In Government Service and Political Life," civil rights, public reform activities, "Race Pride," and "Black Women Speak of Womanhood." Fifteen page bibliographic essay.

235 Lerner, Gerda, ed. *The Female Experience: An American Documentary.* Indianapolis: Bobbs-Merrill, 1977. 509 p.
A collection of documents by American women arranged by topic, ranging from "the personal to the institutional" (introduction); though some are familiar, many were hard to find prior to this volume. The first section focuses on the family, with selections on childhood, marriage, motherhood, being single, housewifery, and old age. The section on women in society deals with education, work (domestic, industrial, and labor organizing), and politics. The third section, on female consciousness, covers women purposely choosing new occupations (E. Blackwell, D. Sampson, E. C. Stanton, E. G. Flynn), woman's right to control her body (rape, birth control, lesbianism), and the search for autonomy. The material is arranged chronologically within the subtopics; each section has an introduction by G. Lerner. A fine collection with a clear sense of the class and racial differences that make up an important part of women's experiences. Includes letters, autobiographies, testimony, speeches, and lectures.

236 Loewenberg, Bert James, and Ruth Bogin, eds. *Black Women in Nineteenth-Century American Life: Their Words, Their Thoughts, Their Feelings.* University Park: Pennsylvania State University Press, 1976. 355 p.
A collection of relatively inaccessible and little-known writings from twenty-four women on family, religion, "social advance," and education. The wide variation in their experiences should prove useful in expanding the reader's awareness of black women's lives.

237 May, Antoinette. *Different Drummers: They Did What They Wanted.* Millbrae, Calif.: Les Femmes, 1976. 156 p., pb.
A "collective biography" of six nonconforming women: V. Woodhull, A.

Earhart, I. Duncan, H. Blavatsky, E. Schumann-Heink, and S. Bernhardt. This is designed to present alternative role models to young girls.

238   Millstein, Beth, and Jeanne Bodin. *We The American Women: A Documentary History.* New York: Jerome S. Ozer, 1977. 331 p., pb.
The authors present a general history beginning with colonial times of women in America (including minority women). After each narrative section short documents from the period such as letters, diaries, newspapers, and fiction are provided. Topics include revolutionary war activity, pioneers, women's rights, Civil War, workers and organizing, suffrage, and women in society to the present. Presents information on individual women, emphasizing for high school readers strong self-reliant images of women. Excellent.

239   Nies, Judith. *Seven Women: Portraits from the American Radical Tradition.* New York: Viking Press, 1977. 236 p.
Biographies of women activists, appropriate for high school readers, which present an alternative model. The women are S. Grimke, H. Tubman, E. C. Stanton, Mother Jones, C. P. Gilman, A. Strong, and D. Day.

240   O'Meara, Walter. *Daughters of the Country: The Women of the Fur Traders and Mountain Men.* New York: Harcourt, Brace and World, 1968. 299 p.
This discussion of the sexual contact between white men and Indian women is based mainly on the journals and letters of the men; ethnocentrism and sexism obscure the scattered useful information.

241   Parker, Gail, ed. *The Ovenbirds: American Women on Womanhood, 1820–1920.* New York: Doubleday, Anchor, 1972. 387 p., pb.
Selections from the letters, memoirs, and fiction of L. H. Sigourney, L. M. Child, A. Grimke, C. Beecher, H. B. Stowe, S. O. Jewett, E. C. Stanton, J. Addams, and C. P. Gilman, with emphasis on how they view themselves, their grandmothers, and their hopes for future generations. Introduction and biographical information by G. Parker.

242   Riegel, Robert E. *American Women: A Story of Social Change.* Rutherford, N.J.: Fairleigh Dickinson University Press, 1970. 376 p.
A history, beginning in the colonial era, that mainly deals with white native-born women. Assumes connection between women's position and industrialization and urbanization. Discusses women and marriage, work, professions, reform. Superficial. Does not treat recent feminist upsurge. Relies a great deal on prescriptive literature.

243   Ryan, Mary P. *Womanhood in America: From Colonial Times to the Present.* New York: Franklin Watts, New Viewpoints, 1975. 496 p., pb.
An excellent, readable history of attitudes toward women, and of women's

attitudes as shown in diaries, fiction, and many other sources. The last half of
the book concerns the twentieth century and covers changes in sexual mores,
consumer activity and women in labor, linking the experiences of women of
different classes.

244 Scott, Ann Firor. *The Southern Lady: From Pedestal to Politics,
1830–1930.* Chicago: University of Chicago Press, 1970. 247 p., pb.
Using diaries, letters, and other sources, Scott describes facets of Southern
women's experiences, particularly the effects of the Civil War on nineteenth-
century women. The author describes the Southern woman's culturally defined
image, traces its effect on women's lives, and characterizes the struggle of
women for freedom and self-determination. Scott discusses white women's
relationship with slaves, and their activities in religion, suffrage, abolition,
and civil rights.

245 Scott, Ann Firor, ed. *The American Woman: Who Was She?* Englewood
Cliffs, N.J.: Prentice-Hall, 1971. 182 p., pb.
Brief writings on women in society: women's work, education, reform,
marriage, and family. Covers approximately 1850 to 1970. Includes government reports, autobiographies, letters, and other sources. Scott provides
background and explanatory comments.

246 *Sex and Equality: Women in America: From Colonial Times to the Twentieth
Century.* New York: Arno Press, 1974. unpaged.
Reprints of H. M. Crocker, M. Fuller, E. H. Heywood, I. C. Craddock, and T.
Veblen. Nineteenth-century selections indicate "changing concepts of the role
of sex in society" (preface). Rarely reprinted, and useful to those using primary
sources.

247 Sklar, Kathryn Kish. *Catharine Beecher: A Study in American Domesticity.* New Haven: Yale University Press, 1973. 356 p., pb.
An important study of one woman and nineteenth-century America,
particularly her role in popularizing the idea that women's place is in the home
through her *Treatise on Domestic Economy.* Contributes to women's, intellectual, and social history.

248 Smith, Page. *Daughters of the Promised Land: Women in American
History: Being an Examination of the Strange History of the Female Sex from the
Beginning to the Present with Special Attention to the Women of America, Illustrated
by Curious Anecdotes and Quotations by Divers Authors, Ancient and Modern.*
Boston: Little, Brown, 1970. 350 p., pb.
This anecdotal history presents women as solely sexual beings, with emphasis
on their roles as daughters and wives. The introductory and concluding
sections are written in anthropological ignorance.

249   Sochen, June. *Herstory: A Woman's View of American History.* Port Washington, New York: Alfred Publishing, 1974. 448 p.
This popularly written personal view of history concentrates on "the similar treatment WASMs (white, Anglo-Saxon, males) gave to all human beings other than themselves, as well as to the environment" (p. ix). Not strictly women's history, except as it views women as victims of oppression.

250   Sochen, June. *Movers and Shakers: American Women Thinkers and Activists, 1900–1970.* New York: Quadrangle/New York Times, 1973. 320 p.
An odd collection of biographical material (F. Hurst, E. Roosevelt, E. G. Flynn, Lady Bird Johnson, among others) provides the frame for this history. The discussion of 1960s "women's lib" (Sochen's term) has the tone of an observer.

251   Sochen, June. *The New Woman: Feminism in Greenwich Village, 1910–1920.* New York: Quadrangle/New York Times, 1972. 175 p.
A descriptive history through discussion of C. Eastman, H. Redman, I. Rauh, N. Boyce, and S. Glaspell. Superficial and lacking in analysis.

252   Sochen, June, ed. *The New Feminism in Twentieth-Century America.* Lexington, Mass.: D. C. Heath, 1971. 208 p., pb.
Writings by feminists from the 1910s and the 1960s, comparing and contrasting views of sexuality, birth control, socialism, and pacifism. Contributors include S. B. Anthony, F. Dell, C. P. Gilman, M. Sanger, C. Eastman, A. Rossi, N. Weisstein, J. Freeman, and A. Hernandez. Each section is preceded by study questions. Not the best collection of these kinds of materials.

253   Spruill, Julia Cherry. *Women's Life and Work in the Southern Colonies.* 1938. Reprint. New York: W. W. Norton, 1972. 426 p., pb.
A classic study of women's public and private lives in the South: their roles in the first settlements, their homes, food, clothes, education, political activities, legal status, and social attitudes. Extensive research is evident in the meticulous detail. Includes a twenty-seven page bibliography; this edition has introduction by Anne Firor Scott.

254   Welter, Barbara. *Dimity Convictions: The American Woman in the Nineteenth Century.* Athens: Ohio University Press, 1976. 230 p.
A collection of previously printed articles on nineteenth-century American women, centered on B. Welter's seminal "The Cult of True Womanhood." Also included are "Coming of Age in America," "Female Complaints," "Anti-Intellectualism and the American Woman," "The Feminization of American Religion," and essays on women novelists who wrote about religious controversy, on A. K. Green's mystery novels, and on M. Fuller. Although

some of these were originally published in the first years of new scholarship on women, they have apparently not been revised, nor is there an introduction to the book as a whole. Nonetheless, a thought-provoking book.

255 Woody, Thomas. *A History of Women's Education in the United States.* 1929. Reprint. New York: Octagon Books, 1966. 2 v.
Presents detailed information on women's education, regionally and chronologically. Includes sections on women as teachers, the rise of female academies, and girls' secondary education. Appendix lists textbooks and courses of study.

United States / Suffrage and Women's Movement

256 Berg, Barbara J. *The Remembered Gate: Origins of American Feminism: The Woman and the City, 1800–1860.* New York: Oxford University Press, 1978. 334 p.
An important contribution to women's and urban studies. Includes information on the different experiences of men and women, the effect of restricted lives, women's interests, feminist concerns beyond obtaining the vote. Well illustrated with examples from a variety of contemporary literature. Concludes that "woman's sense of the oppression of her sex originated in American cities" (p. 7). Twenty-seven page bibliography includes popular songs, sermons, letters and diaries, travelers' accounts, schoolbooks.

257 Coolidge, Olivia. *Women's Rights: The Suffrage Movement in America, 1848–1920.* New York: E. P. Dutton, 1966. 189 p.
Aimed at the high school level, this is a straightforward history of the suffrage movement, told in an anecdotal style. Many fine photographs. Emphasis on the leaders of the movement.

258 Cooper, James L., and Sheila McIsaac Cooper, eds. *The Roots of American Feminist Thought.* Boston: Allyn and Bacon, 1973. 298 p., pb.
Selections from the writings of M. Wollstonecraft, S. Grimke, M. Fuller, J. S. Mill, C. P. Gilman, M. Sanger, S. LaFollette. Introduction to each reading contains extensive biographical and historical material.

259 Flexner, Eleanor. *Century of Struggle: The Woman's Rights Movement in the United States.* 1959. Reprint. New York: Atheneum, 1973. 384 p., pb.
A fascinating, readable history of the women's rights movement. Includes coverage of labor activity, black women, and also a note on the opposition. Details unknown as well as well-known women's activities, women's struggles for education, and the growth of women's clubs. Women's rights is seen in its full scope, not simply as suffrage struggle, although that is discussed in its full complexity. A classic.

260   Gluck, Sherna. *From Parlor to Prison: Five American Suffragists Talk about Their Lives.* New York: Random House, Vintage Books, 1976. 285 p., pb.
After an introduction to set the scene, Gluck allows five women to tell of their experiences, which range from giving tea parties and talking about suffrage to picketing Woodrow Wilson's White House and spending a month in jail. The women include a birth control activist, a federal lobbyist, an accomplished public lecturer, a businesswoman, and an active socialist.

261   Grimes, Alan P. *The Puritan Ethic and Woman Suffrage.* New York: Oxford University Press, 1967. 157 p.
An investigation into why women's suffrage was so much more successful in the West than in the rest of the U.S. Grimes's thesis is that "the constituency granting woman suffrage was composed of those who also supported prohibition and immigration restriction and felt woman suffrage would further their enactment" (p. xii). A contribution to frontier history, women's history, and American history generally.

262   Irwin, Inez Haynes. *The Story of the Woman's Party.* 1921. Reprint. New York: Kraus Reprint, 1971. 486 p.
A political history of the end of the struggle for women's voting rights, by a participant. Focuses on the organization and activities of the Woman's Party.

263   Kraditor, Aileen S. *The Ideas of the Woman Suffrage Movement, 1890–1920.* 1965. Reprint. New York: Doubleday, Anchor, 1971. 262 p., pb.
Based on research into the writings of the national leaders of the National American Woman Suffrage Association (NAWSA) and the Woman's Party, legislative testimony, and NAWSA's published proceedings. Discusses the history of suffragist organization, rationale of antisuffragism, two major types of suffragist argument, women suffrage and religion, women and the home, immigration and labor, the "southern question," political parties, and suffragist tactics. This scholarly study also includes an appendix of brief biographies of twenty-six suffragists.

264   Kraditor, Aileen S., ed. *Up from the Pedestal: Selected Writings in the History of American Feminism.* Chicago: Quadrangle Press, 1968. 372 p., pb.
A variety of documents, the first by A. Bradstreet and the last a statement of purpose of the National Organization for Women. Introductory essay on feminist historiography. Documents focus on a representation of the principal emphases of the feminist movement in each period.

265   Melder, Keith E. *Beginnings of Sisterhood: The American Woman's Rights Movement, 1800–1850.* New York: Schocken Books, 1977. 199 p.
After outlining attitudes toward women, Melder presents material on women's activities that contributed to feminist concerns. Topics include education, female seminaries, female networks, women in reform movements, local

women's societies, antislavery activities, political activity on the "woman question." The conclusion shows the development of the women's rights movements from these earlier experiences. Important contribution, deals with period not extensively covered in most other women's histories.

266 Morgan, David. *Suffragists and Democrats: The Politics of Woman Suffrage in America.* East Lansing: Michigan State University Press, 1972. 255 p.
A study of the struggle for the vote as it occurred in the national political arena, particularly the congressional fight. Examines some changes that led to acceptance of women voting (increasing educational parity with men, higher female employment, legal reform, general political trends) and discusses the conflict within Congress and the ratification of the amendment. Includes nineteen page bibliography.

267 O'Neill, William L. *Everyone Was Brave: A History of Feminism in America.* Rev. ed. New York: Quadrangle/New York Times, 1973. 379 p., pb.
Discusses the origins of the feminist movement, the growth of its principal demand for women's suffrage, women's organizations (General Federation of Women's Clubs, National Women's Trade Union League, and others), ten prominent feminist leaders, women reformists in the Progressive era, their involvement in trade unions, the events in the women's movement during World War I (including the Woman's Peace Party and nationalists). Discusses the role of the various prominent organizations and the postsuffrage movement; includes an afterword on feminism in the late 1960s.

268 Papachristou, Judith. *Women Together: A History in Documents of the Women's Movement in the United States.* New York: Alfred A. Knopf, 1976. 273 p., pb.
This Ms. collection contains material from the 1830s through the 1960s and 1970s and is arranged chronologically. Most of the documents are from the suffrage movement; material from Women's Christian Temperance Union and other women's associations is also included. Documents are linked by brief explanatory sections.

269 Scott, Anne F., and Andrew M. Scott. *One Half the People: The Fight for Woman Suffrage.* Philadelphia: J. B. Lippincott, 1975. 173 p., pb.
The first half is a straightforward history of the suffrage movement, beginning with a brief look at the seventeenth and eighteenth centuries and the assumptions of property holding on which voting rights were based and proceeding through ratification of the Nineteenth Amendment. The second half presents illustrative documents, including the Seneca Falls Declaration, letters and statements by some of the leaders (E. C. Stanton, C. C. Catt, and others), excerpts from congressional debate and testimony, and court decisions. A compilation of material useful for studying this aspect of the political history of America.

270 Sinclair, Andrew. *The Better Half: The Emancipation of the American Woman.* New York: Harper and Row, 1965. 401 p.
An historical survey of women's struggle for emancipation. Description of colonial social conditions, early feminist literature, early suffragist personalities, legal changes, education, clothing, "ladies," working women, professionals, religion, writers, conflict over the Fifteenth Amendment, opposition from the churches, immigrants, the English experience, the narrowing to a quest for the vote, and trade unions. Deals with the complexity of regional and class differences, though focus is on prominent women. Published prior to recent research on women, rendering much of this out of date.

271 Stevens, Doris. *Jailed for Freedom.* New York: Boni and Liveright, 1920. 388 p.
A history of the activities of militant American suffragists in their campaign for women's franchise (1913–1919), by a participant. Many photographs.

International / General

272 *African Studies Review* 18, no. 3 (December 1975). "Women in Africa."
This special issue, edited by E. Bay and N. Hafkin, contains articles on Senegal female elites (D. Barthel), invisibility and political activity (J. O'Barr), Guinea-Bissau (S. Urdang), weddings in Mombasa (M. Strobel), women in development (Human Resources Development Division, U.N. Economic Commission for Africa), women's loss of power in Ghana (C. Oppong, C. Okali, D. Houghton), farmer's and weaver's wives in Ethiopia (J. Olmstead), and women's organization in Kenya (A. Wipper), and book reviews. Good range of coverage of women's economic and political activities throughout the continent.

273 Allendorf, Marlis. *Women in Socialist Society.* New York: International Publishers. 1975. 219 p.
A history of women in Russia, East Germany, and other Eastern European countries that emphasizes women at work and women in love. The text is sometimes stilted and dogmatic; the photographs are the most useful part of this book.

274 *Annals of the American Academy of Political and Social Science* 143, no. 232 (May 1929). "Women in the Modern World."
Includes articles on the women's movement, women's contributions to the home and their work in industry, public achievements, social attitudes, integration of work and family care.

275 Asthana, Pratima. *Women's Movement in India.* Delhi: Vikas Publishing House, 1974. 175 p.

Brief overview of women in Indian history, effect of British colonialism, male Indian reformers and the women's "cause," women leaders and organizers, growth of women's movement in twentieth century, Indian women in politics (including the suffrage movement), and education. Much of book is brief biography or history of organizations, with an evaluation section in each chapter. There is little mention of those women who were not active in the movement in any way, and the effect the activities of the more privileged had on their lives. Includes seven page bibliography.

276   Bergman, Arlene Eisen. *Women of Vietnam.* San Francisco: People's Press, 1974. 223 p., pb.
Written in a popular style, this book covers a wide range of topics concerning Vietnamese women. Begins with a brief historical survey. Topics discussed: the politics of rape and prostitution, the effects of chemical warfare on future generations, women political prisoners, women in the army and in the liberated areas. Ends with a discussion of what socialism has meant for these women.

277   Bernstein, Hilda. *For Their Triumphs and for Their Tears: Women in Apartheid South Africa.* London: International Defence and Aid Fund, 1975. 72 p., pb.
An overview, by a white woman who was herself detained by the South African government, of the special effects apartheid has on African women, their hardships, and their resistance. Includes brief biographies of activist women.

278   Boxer, C. R. *Mary and Misogyny: Women in Iberian Expansion Overseas 1415–1815, Some Facts, Fancies, and Personalities.* London: Gerald Duckworth, 1975. 142 p.
A "tentative essay" by a widely published historian of Iberian expansion. Chapters are titled "Morocco, West Africa and the Atlantic Islands;" "Spanish and Portuguese America;" "Portuguese Asia and the Spanish Philippines;" "The Cult of Mary and the Practice of Misogyny." A useful introduction to and outline of the limited available material although it is history by anecdote for the most part, with no larger analysis.

279   Broyelle, Claudie. *Women's Liberation in China.* Atlantic Highlands, N.J.: Humanities Press, 1977. 174 p.
An analysis of women's position in revolutionary China, based primarily on Broyelle's November 1971 visit to China. Incorporates personal narratives of Chinese women interviewed, Broyelle's observations, extensive historical background, and comparison with French society in examination of social labor, the socialization of housework, the family and motherhood, children's liberation, and sexuality in China. Emphasizes descriptive analysis versus an

assessment of women's status. Critically views China's progress toward sexual equality, pointing out presence of sex inequality in Chinese power structure. Scholarly and informative.

280 *Bulletin of Concerned Asian Scholars* 7, no. 1 (January–March 1975). Special issue on Asian women, which includes V. Schwarcz on Lu Hsun; J. and S. MacKinnon on A. Smedley; a story by A. Smedley; J. Price on women and leadership in the Chinese communist movement (1921–1945); N. Diamond on collectivization, kinship, and rural women's status; P. Andors on social revolution and women's emancipation; G. Omvedt on class, caste, and women's liberation in India; S. Mody and S. Mhatre on sexual class in India; poems and songs about Indian women revolutionaries; and a brief biography of K. Chattopadhyaya by B. Cobb. A useful and unique collection.

281 *Canadian Journal of African Studies* 6, no. 2 (1972). "African Women." Sixteen articles (three in French) on African women and change. Excellent collection that includes "Sitting on a Man" (J. Van Allen), roles of women (A. Wipper), associations and mobility among W. African women (K. Little), Hausa women in Nigeria (J. Barkow), Ghanaian women (M. Greenstreet), Tanzanian women (M. Mbilinyi), women in Botswana (R. Mookodi), and conjugal behavior (J. Pool). Basic collection.

282 Carroll, Berenice A., ed. *Liberating Women's History: Theoretical and Critical Essays.* Urbana: University of Illinois Press, 1976. 434 p.
Essays primarily concerned with historiographical issues, and studies or surveys that discuss theoretical problems. Includes critiques of Engels and of M. Beard, articles on sexism in American historical writing, the problem of women's history, gynecology and ideology, education, German nineteenth-century feminism, women's trade union leagues, Latina liberation, black women, Algerian cultural liberation, matriarchy, medieval women, nuns in colonial Mexico, sex and class in early America, Weimar women, women's work and social order. The final section contains several articles on new directions and methodology in women's history. Altogether a stimulating collection which deals with basic theoretical questions and provides important new information on international women's history.

283 Cook, Ramsay, and Wendy Mitchinson, eds. *The Proper Sphere: Woman's Place in Canadian Society.* Toronto: Oxford University Press, 1976. 334 p., pb.
A documentary collection covering the topics of "women's sphere," legal rights, education, work, organizations, morality, and suffrage from the 1850s to World War I. Includes magazine articles, speeches, and lectures. Brief introductions to book and to each section. Interesting collection of solely Canadian materials.

284   Croll, Elisabeth. *The Women's Movement in China: A Selection of Readings, 1949–1973.* London: Anglo-Chinese Educational Institute, 1974. 115 p., pb.
Brief articles on "the structure, working methods and goals of the women's movement in China" post-1949. Deals with theoretical and practical concerns, from Chinese sources (especially daily newspapers and Women's Federation publications). Not always easily readable due to Chinese style and translation, but informative and useful for beginning discussion of various issues concerning socialist feminism. Arranged by topic: separate organizations, role in family, role in society, and ideology.

285   Curtin, Katie. *Women in China.* New York: Pathfinder Press, 1975. 95 p., pb.
A brief, popularly written review of the changing status of women in China, which includes material on the historical oppression of women, their role in the Party and politics, in education, in the work force, and in management positions. Discusses the issues of abortion, birth control, and sexuality. Acknowledges advances of the Chinese revolution while criticizing continued limitations on women's equality. Curtin sees the continued presence of bureaucratic bourgeois leaders as the major roadblock to sexual equality.

286   Davin, Delia. *Woman-Work: Women and the Party in Revolutionary China.* Oxford: Clarendon Press, 1976. 244 p.
An important, well-written contribution to the historical literature on Chinese women. Focuses on women's participation and activities in the revolution. The first chapter presents material on the anti-Japanese and civil war period, providing information on some early "communist experimentation." Other topics discussed in depth are women's organizations, marriage and family, rural women and urban women; most of the study deals with the 1950s. Excellent and informative.

287   Hafkin, Nancy J., and Edna G. Bay, eds. *Women in Africa: Studies in Social and Economic Change.* Stanford: Stanford University Press, 1976. 306 p.
An interdisciplinary collection of articles on women in Africa, "concerned with women's participation in activities beyond the closed circle of child care or household maintenance" (p. 5). Introduction ties articles together and supplies summaries of findings. Topics are women entrepreneurs in eighteenth-century Senegal (G. Brooks, Jr.), Igbo women (Nigeria, K. Okonjo), Igbo Women's War (J. Van Allen), Ga women (Ghana, C. Robertson), market women of Abidjan (Ivory Coast, B. C. Lewis), women as spirit mediums in East Africa (I. Berger), women's associations in Mombasa (Kenya, M. Strobel) and in Freetown (Sierra Leone, F. Steady), women and economic change (Ghana and Mozambique, L. Mullings), and women in cooperative villages in Tanzania (J. L. Brain).

288 Hahner, June E., ed. *Women in Latin American History: Their Lives and Views.* UCLA Latin American Studies Series, Vol. 34. Los Angeles: University of California, Latin American Center, 1976. 181 p., pb.
Selections from the letters, diaries, and novels of Latin American women, from the 1550s to the present. Suffers from an obvious bias in favor of literate women, though two of Oscar Lewis's tapes are included. Attempts to cover politics and feminism as well as give a view of everyday life.

289 Johnston, Jean. *Wilderness Women: Canada's Forgotten History.* Toronto: Peter Martin, 1973. 242 p.
The stories of eight women who were Canadian pioneers. Written in popular style; perhaps most suited to high school or lower level. This is a source on women who are usually omitted from histories.

290 *Latin American Perspectives* 4, nos. 1, 2 (1977). "Women and Class Struggle."
Eleven aticles by social scientists on class analysis of Latin American women. Topics include theoretical issues involved in study, women and labor, imperialism, dependency, and production. Articles view oppression of women as direct result of class society and its correlates. Good articles on theory and Cuban, Mexican, Peruvian, Venezuelan, and Argentinian women.

291 Mandel, William M. *Soviet Women.* New York: Doubleday, Anchor, 1975. 350 p., pb.
An informative book that frequently compares Soviet women's experiences and conditions to those of American women. Chapters on prerevolutionary history, women in the revolution, postrevolution changes, education, individual women in a variety of occupations, sectors of "women's work" and protective legislation, professionals, arts and sports, agricultural work, and minorities. Provides examples of women's writings on women's position, family patterns, sexuality, retirement, politics, other communist countries (Cuba, North Vietnam, China, Eastern Europe). Records many conversations with Soviet women as well as personal experiences from Mandel's many trips to the USSR. Includes seven page bibliography.

292 Massell, Gregory. *The Surrogate Proletariat: Moslem Women and Revolutionary Strategies in Soviet Central Asia (1919–1929).* Princeton: Princeton University Press, 1974. 390 p.
An historical and political analysis that emphasizes the role of women in the revolutionary struggle. This scholarly study focuses on the traditional family and kinship system and the relationship of their breakdown to the mobilization of women.

293 Matheson, Gwen, ed. *Women in the Canadian Mosaic.* Toronto: Peter Martin, 1976. 353 p.

Focuses on Canadian women's history and present status. The historical articles include material on N. McClung (an outspoken Canadian feminist of the first part of the twentieth century); Canadian suffragists; French-Canadian women in Quebec; and the Voice of Women, a group of antibomb and antiwar activists. The articles on aspects of the present discuss the churches, immigrants, "farm wives," schools, women's studies, university women, women and unions, women writers, artists, politics, and the feminist movement. Much of the latter section is based on Matheson's personal experiences (as writer, political activist, other occupations).

294   *NACLA's Latin America and Empire Report* 9, no. 6 (September 1975). This issue contains three articles concerning women: "Aspects of the Condition of Women's Labor," by I. Larquia and J. Dumoulin, a wordy, hard to follow, Marxist analysis of women's oppression; "Chile: The Feminine Side of the Coup or When Bourgeois Women Take to the Streets," by M. Mattelart, an interesting discussion of how reactionaries made political use of these women; and "Women in the Chilean Resistance," by C. Castillo, a speech given in Quebec in April 1975.

295   Okamura, Masu. *Women's Status in Changing Japan.* Tokyo: International Society for Educational Information, 1973. 76 p.
An analysis of women and home, work, public life, and education in the recent history of Japan. Compares "official status," primarily legal codes, with "facts" of daily life. Discrepancy centers on relative lack of discrimination in the laws versus the generally inferior position of women evidenced in labor, education, and participation in politics. However, there is an increasing awareness of this discrepancy, and increasing efforts aimed at eliminating it from the social, political, and economic spheres of Japanese life. Japanese legal codes are dealt with thoroughly. Scholarly use of government statistics. Contains many informative photographs.

296   Paulson, Ross Evans. *Women's Suffrage and Prohibition: A Comparative Study of Equality and Social Control.* Glenview, Ill.: Scott, Foresman, 1973. 212 p., pb.
A thoroughly researched and well-written commentary and history of two frequently aligned issues. International perspective: U.S., England, New Zealand and Australia, Scandinavia, France. Theme is that "the 'woman question' and the 'temperance question' of the nineteenth and early twentieth centuries were aspects of the debates on the meaning of equality and the nature of democracy" (p. 7). Uses secondary historical sources and literature to good advantage. Extensive annotated footnotes.

297   Randall, Margaret. *Cuban Women Now: Interviews with Cuban Women.* Toronto: Women's Press and Dumont Press, 1974. 375 p., pb.
Useful introduction and interviews with a wide variety of Cuban women point

out the gains and changes made in Cuba since the revolution. An historical perspective on women's involvement in the various resistance movements. Women discuss ways in which they are now involved in Cuban society, men's attitudes, older generation's attitudes, other limits to rate of change. Excellent for discussion of relationships between socialism and feminism, and what socialism has meant for women in one country.

298 Sidel, Ruth. *Women and Child Care in China: A Firsthand Report.* Baltimore: Penguin, 1972. 201 p., pb.
After a brief discussion of women's prerevolutionary position in China, Sidel describes the new legal status of women; birth control; childcare and education, based on her visits to nurseries and kindergartens; and the similarities and differences of childrearing practices in China, Israel, and the Soviet Union. Includes many photographs.

299 *Signs* 2, no. 1 (Autumn 1976).
A special issue on women in China, introduced by M. B. Young. Articles include P. S. Robb on women in the early and mid Ch'ing, I. Eber on women in recent Chinese fiction, L. Kung on factory work and women in Taiwan, M. Sheridan on young women leaders, and P. Andors on the case of women and the politics of Chinese development from 1960 to 1966. Also included are reviews of recent books on Chinese women, and two relevant archival contributions.

300 Smedley, Agnes. *Portraits of Chinese Women in Revolution.* Edited by Jan MacKinnon and Steve MacKinnon. Old Westbury, N.Y.: Feminist Press, 1976. 204 p., pb.
Short pieces on Chinese women in the 1920s and 1930s that present extensive information on the conditions of women during the revolution, as cadre and bourgeois women. Informed throughout by a strong class and feminist consciousness. The editors include an introduction on China and A. Smedley, and an afterword by F. Howe on Smedley the writer.

301 Snow, Helen Foster. *Women in Modern China.* The Hague: Mouton, 1967. 264 p.
Wide-ranging study, beginning with the T'aip'ing Rebellion; discusses women in the family, women and Christianity, education, the Kuomintang. Includes many interesting autobiographies. Sometimes reads like a travel account; little analysis.

302 Swidler, Leonard. *Women in Judaism: The Status of Women in Formative Judaism.* Metuchen, N.J.: Scarecrow Press, 1976. 242 p.
An historical study of women's status and roles in early Judaism. Attitudes of major Jewish groups towards women, women in relation to Cult and Torah, women in society, and women and sex are investigated in this discussion of

some cultural origins of inequality. Thorough discussion; assumes some knowledge of Jewish history.

303   Wolf, Margery, and Roxane Witke, eds. *Women in Chinese Society.* Stanford: Stanford University Press, 1975. 315 p.
Collection of papers originally presented at a 1973 conference. Contributors and topics: J. F. Handlin, sixteenth-century women's literacy; M. B. Rankin, the emergence of women at the end of the Ch'ing; M. Topley, marriage resistance; A. Wolf, demography; M. Wolf, suicide; Y. Feuerwerker, writers in the 1920s and 1930s; R. Witke, Chiang Ch'ing; E. Ahern, power and pollution; E. Johnson, childbearing and social change; D. Davin, rural women. Much useful information.

304   Young, Marilyn B., ed. *Women in China: Studies in Social Change and Feminism.* Michigan Papers in Chinese Studies, no. 15. Ann Arbor: University of Michigan, Center for Chinese Studies, 1973. 259 p., pb.
A very good collection by feminist sinologists, including R. Witke, N. Milton, S. Leith, J. Salaff, Soong Ching-ling, Lu Yu-lan, J. Merkle, J. Barrett, and N. Diamond. Addresses question dealing with women's liberation in a revolutionary society, surveys historical and social effects (fertility and families), offers personal observations on Chinese women's participation, and discusses American and Chinese women's liberation.

International / Europe

305   Adam, Ruth. *A Woman's Place: 1910–1975.* London: Chatto and Windus, 1975. 224 p.
Simplistic discussion of women in England, particularly from the vantage point of attitudes. Fiction sources are widely quoted. Topics include women working during World War I, education, women in Parliament, the depression, World War II women in uniform, teenagers in the 1960s. Descriptive rather than analytic.

306   Adburgham, Alison. *Women in Print: Writing Women and Women's Magazines from the Restoration to the Accession of Victoria.* London: George Allen and Unwin, 1972. 302 p.
A descriptive history of the variety of publications that European women produced: novels, plays, and magazines; includes a chronological list. Useful in illuminating part of women's forgotten history, as well as offering a guide to some historical sources on women.

307   Backer, Dorothy Anne Liot. *Precious Women.* New York: Basic Books, 1974. 308 p.
A social history of seventeenth-century upper-class French women—those called "précieuses." Written in an anecdotal and sometimes flowery manner

with no scholarly pretensions—nonetheless, informative about the period. Written from a feminist perspective, though the wording sometimes grates (e.g., girlfriend). Much of the book deals with individual women.

308 Bainton, Roland H. *Women of the Reformation in France and England.* Minneapolis: Augsburg, 1973. 287 p., pb.
Biographies of women of the Reformation, including Marguerite de Navarre, Catherine of Aragon, Anne Boleyn, Elizabeth I, and others, through which other information on the period is presented.

309 Bainton, Roland H. *Women of the Reformation in Germany and Italy.* Minneapolis: Augsburg, 1971. 279 p., pb.
Biographies of women of the Catholic and Protestant reform movements in the early sixteenth century.

310 Banks, J. A., and Olive Banks. *Feminism and Family Planning in Victorian England.* Liverpool: Liverpool University Press, 1964. 142 p., pb.
A thorough investigation into the relationship between the feminist and family planning movements. Includes information on attitudes toward sexuality, and on the model of the ideal wife and mother. An interesting study, approaches feminism from a different perspective.

311 Bell, Susan Groag, ed. *Women: From the Greeks to the French Revolution.* Belmont, Calif.: Wadsworth, 1973. 313 p., pb.
An anthology that deals with the historic position of women in Plato, Aristotle, Christianity, the Bible, medieval nunneries, St. Thomas Aquinas, Chaucer, Erasmus, Juan Luis Vives, the Reformation, and the Enlightenment. Each section includes contemporary texts and analytic essays, and Bell provides background information as well. A useful collection; nicely done and includes a twenty-four page annotated bibliography.

312 Branca, Patricia. *Silent Sisterhood: Middle Class Women in the Victorian Home.* London: Croom Helm, 1975. 170 p.
History of middle-class Victorian women with a special focus on their roles as homemakers and mothers, and their struggles for better health and birth control. Uses modernization and "modern women" as key concepts. The book is limited by Branca's sources, which are primarily prescriptive manuals of the era, though it does contain valuable information.

313 Bridenthal, Renate, and Claudia Koonz, eds. *Becoming Visible: Women in European History.* Boston: Houghton Mifflin, 1977. 510 p., pb.
A collection of twenty articles, beginning with a theoretical overview, "Women in Egalitarian Societies," by E. Leacock. Includes, chronologically, essays on Crete and Sumer (R. Rohrlich-Leavitt), classical era (M. Arthur), courtly love and witchcraft (E. W. Monter), Renaissance (J. Kelly-Gadol),

preindustrial capitalism (R. T. Vaun), French Revolution (R. Graham), working-class women in the Industrial Revolution (M. L. McDougall), women's work and industrialization (T. M. McBride), leisured women in nineteenth-century England and France (B. C. Pope), international sisterhood (E. F. Hurwitz), Russian populists (B. Engel), Russian revolution and after (B. G. Rosenthal), Spanish anarchism (T. Kaplan), between the world wars (R. Bridenthal), Nazi Germany (C. Koonz), and family models of the future (A. Michel), among others. Each article is introduced with a synopsis which connects it with others in the collection. As well as ably presenting facets of women in history and women's history, these selections are alert to the economic and class divisions that also governed women's experiences.

314 Cuddeford, Gladys. *Women and Society: From Victorian Times to the Present Day.* London: Hamish Hamilton, 1967. 120 p.
A superficial account of Victorian women, the struggle for suffrage, women at work, women and the arts, and women in politics.

315 Dunbar, Janet. *The Early Victorian Woman: Some Aspects of Her Life (1837–57).* London: George G. Harrap, 1953. 192 p.
A history concerned with the material details of everyday life: marriage, family, houses, servants, shops, food and housekeeping, fashion, leisure, amusements, holidays, and travel. Other topics include education, women's work, outstanding women, and women's rights. Good source for details; not analytical.

316 Evans, Richard J. *The Feminist Movement in Germany 1894–1933.* Beverly Hills: Sage, 1976. 310 p.
An overview of the women's movement as part of German liberalism. Includes middle-class women's rights in Imperial Germany; social welfare to social reform; police, prostitution, and repression in Hamburg; suffrage movement; changes in morality; intellectual history and women; antifeminism; World War I and the peace movement; and the collapse of the women's movement. A scholarly and important contribution to German history and women's history.

317 Kamm, Josephine. *Rapiers and Battleaxes: The Women's Movement and Its Aftermath.* London: George Allen and Unwin, 1966. 240 p.
An anecdotal history of the women's rights movement in Britain that emphasizes personalities; includes material from 1792 to the 1960s, with a chapter on women in World War II.

318 Middleton, Lucy, ed. *Women in the Labour Movement: The British Experience.* London: Croom Helm; and Totowa, N.J.: Rowman and Littlefield, 1977. 221 p.
A collection of nine articles on historical aspects of women and labor politics, and the movement today, primarily from a Labour party perspective. Specific

topics include Labour women and the social services, the suffrage struggle, internationalism, cooperatives, the Labour party today, modern trade unions, and women in Parliament and government. Generally an informative overview of women and official labor-oriented political activity with little analysis.

319 O'Faolain, Julia, and Laura Martines, eds. *Not in God's Image*. London: Temple Smith, 1973. 362 p.
Historical readings concerning women in European societies from early Greece to the mid-1800s. The editors have provided extensive notes throughout, placing the documents in historical perspective. This makes for choppy reading, however, as each selection is very brief (only a paragraph or so). Selections and their notes are in different type; many illustrations. Includes material on laws and customs, education, religion, work, rural women, prostitutes, socialists in France, and salons.

320 Pomeroy, Sarah B. *Goddesses, Whores, Wives, and Slaves: Women in Classical Antiquity*. New York: Schocken Books, 1975. 265 p.
An important text dealing with women in ancient Greece and Rome. Discusses goddesses, Homeric epics, private life in classical Athens, images of women in literature, Hellenistic women, Roman matrons, lower-class Roman women, and women and Roman religion. Vital to a better understanding of that period.

321 Power, Eileen. *Medieval Women*. Edited by M. M. Postan. Cambridge: Cambridge University Press, 1975. 112 p.
A newly edited collection of Power's popular essays on medieval women. The topics addressed include medieval ideas about women, working women, education, and nunneries. The essays were apparently given as talks in the 1920s; they are designed for the general public, as are the many illustrations in this volume.

322 Rover, Constance. *Love, Morals and the Feminists*. London: Routledge and Kegan Paul, 1970. 183 p.
Beginning with women and the French Revolution, Rover investigates the interconnections between changes in public morality and the movement for women's rights. Information is mainly French and English, with some American. Emphasis is on those who left written records; discusses issues such as birth control, divorce, prostitution. Includes chapters on Josephine Butler and the Contagious Diseases Act, white slavery, A. Besant, and the Pankhursts. A general review; no solid analysis.

323 Rowbotham, Sheila. *Hidden from History: Rediscovering Women in History from the 17th Century to the Present*. New York: Random House, Pantheon Books, 1974. 183 p., pb.

Popularly written history of women in England up to the 1930s. Covers a wide range of concerns, particularly women in the workplace (including their homes), the development of feminist thought and the suffrage movement, and the effect of sexual mores and birth control practices on male/female relationships. A good Marxist interpretation of women in history; connects personal, public, political segments of women's lives. Good introductory essay on the nature of feminist history.

324   Scott, Hilda. *Does Socialism Liberate Women?: Experiences from Eastern Europe.* Boston: Beacon Press, 1974. 240 p., pb.
A well-written, instructive, objective discussion of the Czechoslovakian experience—includes sections on women in the history of socialism in Europe, statistics on women workers, information on birth control and on nursery schools and collective housekeeping tasks. Scott's argument (though she is not explicit here) is that both socialism and feminism are necessary and that it is important to struggle for both, but one should not assume that socialism will liberate women—although as she explains, it certainly provides for women's rights in a way capitalism does not.

325   Stenton, Doris Mary. *The English Woman in History.* New York: Macmillan, 1957. 363 p.
Beginning with Anglo-Saxon accounts, and ending in 1869 with J. S. Mill's *The Subjection of Women,* Stenton discusses women as they "lived and worked in the England of their day." Extensive research using letters, wills, laws, and other sources. Inevitably, particularly with the earlier periods, much of the information deals with individuals who left records. Not very analytic; presents interesting specific information.

326   Stephenson, Jill. *Women in Nazi Society.* London: Croom Helm, 1975. 223 p.
A thorough and scholarly inquiry into the period between the wars in Germany. Topics include emancipation and reaction in the 1920s, marriage and motherhood, birth control, employment, education, professionals. Also includes an overview of the 1930s. Adds to knowledge of German history and European women.

327   Vicinus, Martha, ed. *Suffer and Be Still: Women in the Victorian Age.* Bloomington: Indiana University Press, 1972. 239 p., pb.
Scholarly articles on a variety of aspects of Victorian women's lives: the roles of governess, women in the theater, menstruation, women as artists (examples are included), prostitution and venereal disease, working-class British women (1890–1914), Ruskin versus Mill (from K. Millett's *Sexual Politics*), femininity and sexual evolution, models of femininity. Includes a thirty page annotated bibliography on women in England, 1815–1914. A coherent collection on a special topic.

328 *Women in a Changing World: The Dynamic Story of the International Council of Women since 1888.* London: Routledge and Kegan Paul, 1966. 360 p. The official history of the International Council of Women, including information on standing committees, international groups, and ICW presidents.

Economic History

329 Abbott, Edith. *Women in Industry: A Study in American Economic History.* 1910. Reprint. New York: Source Book Press, 1970. 409 p. A classic study of women in American industry, from colonial times to the beginning of the twentieth century, with emphasis on the period of transition when factories were being established. Includes information on specific industries: cotton milling, early mill working, boot manufacturing, cigar making, clothing, printing; and material on women's wages, and public opinion of working women. Appendixes include information on child labor pre-1870, census statistics, wages in the cotton mills, early corporation rules and regulations, lists of women's occupations, and a seven page bibliography.

330 Baker, Elizabeth Faulkner. *Technology and Woman's Work.* New York: Columbia University Press, 1964. 460 p. A descriptive history, beginning about 1800. Provides information on factory and farm work, teaching and other white-collar jobs, with emphasis on material goods that affected women's work (such as the typewriter and the telephone). Baker also discusses sexual discrimination in labor, labor legislation, World War II, and education (teaching methods).

331 Baxandall, Rosalyn; Linda Gordon; and Susan Reverby; eds. *America's Working Women: A Documentary History—1600 to the Present.* New York: Random House, 1976. 408 p., pb. A documentary collection arranged chronologically; begins with a selection on Ojibwa women. Includes material on work in the home, slavery, factory work, industrial dissent and protest, pioneer women, the effects of industrialization and worker's response, migrants and immigrants, working-class power, strikes and other struggles, women's class consciousness, the depression, war work, postwar controversy over working women, the double working day of the present, and the continuing struggle. The selections cover a wide range of work and women. Most are written by women: personal accounts, letters to newspapers, analytic selections (e.g., M. Davies on clerical workers). The editors provide brief and useful introductions to many sections. An excellent source, with most selections difficult to obtain elsewhere.

332 Bird, Caroline. *Enterprising Women.* New York: W. W. Norton, 1976. 256 p. A highly readable history of self-reliant American women involved in business and other economic activity from colonial times to the present. Interesting biographical vignettes on such women as M. K. Goddard, E. Pickney, A. Adams, C. Beecher, D. Dix, E. Blackwell, L. Pinkham, K. Gibbs, and K. Graham. Descriptive rather than analytic, but ably documents contributions of women.

333 Boone, Gladys. *The Women's Trade Union Leagues in Great Britain and the United States of America.* New York: Columbia University Press, 1942. 283 p.
Historical study of organizations that were part of both the feminist and labor movements. Thoroughly researched, with much information, particularly on the labor movement in general and on relations of women with male-dominated unions.

334 Brandeis, Louis D., and Josephine Goldmark. *Women in Industry.* 1907. Reprint. New York: Arno Press and New York Times, 1969. 113 p.
Presents the legal material relevant to the 1908 Supreme Court decision on hours laws for working women. Documents the danger of not limiting women's hours to ten or fewer per day.

335 Brownlee, W. Elliot, and Mary M. Brownlee, eds. *Women in the American Economy: A Documentary History, 1675 to 1929.* New Haven: Yale University Press, 1976. 350 p., pb.
Historical writings by and about women working, including diaries, letters, fiction, essays, government reports and testimonies, from colonial times to around 1930. Although some of the selections are interesting, many are readily available elsewhere. The arrangement of this book makes it very difficult to find particular articles, as the editors' introductory comments tend to merge with the selections. Some incongruous selections, such as Mother Jones speaking against suffrage, Herbert Hoover on consumerism.

336 Cantor, Milton, and Bruce Laurie, eds. *Class, Sex, and the Woman Worker.* Westport, Conn.: Greenwood Press, 1977. 253 p.
A collection of ten essays previously prepared for conferences and publication elsewhere, with an introduction by C. F. Ware. The topics include the study of urban women (S. J. Kleinberg), Lowell mill workers' protests (T. Dublin), New England mill women (L. Vogel), women workers in mid-nineteenth-century New York City (C. Groneman), Italian women and work (V. Yans-McLaughlin), Italian-American women in New York City, 1900 to 1950 (M. Cohen), Jewish women union organizers (A. Kessler-Harris), unions in Cripple Creek, 1894 to 1904 (E. Jameson), Women's Trade Union League and feminism (R. M. Jacoby), and sisterhood and class conflict in the New York Women's Trade Union League (N. S. Dye). An excellent collection of some of the best recent research on American women workers.

337 Clark, Alice. *Working Life of Women in the Seventeenth Century.* 1919. Reprint. New York: Augustus M. Kelley, 1968.
A classic investigation into women's work in the 1600s from a socialist point of view. Discussed by occupation: "capitalists," agriculture, textiles, crafts and trades, and professions. Detailed information from letters, diaries, and other accounts of the period makes this a very useful source.

338 Dexter, Elisabeth A. *Career Women of America, 1176–1840.* Francestown, N.H.: M. Jones, 1950. 262 p.
Continues discussion in *Colonial Women of Affairs,* with material on teachers; medical workers (midwives, nurses, etc.); religious workers; readers, singers, dancers, other entertainers; writers, printers, journalists; tavernkeepers; keepers of small shops in homes; clerks; those in outside work (on the frontier, farms, and plantations); and textile workers. Dexter's intent is to investigate the opportunities such careers offered to women, and the new choices and restrictions pre- and post-1776.

339 Dexter, Elisabeth A. *Colonial Women of Affairs.* New York: Houghton Mifflin, 1931. 223 p.
A descriptive discussion of women workers, pre-1776, by occupation: tavernkeepers, merchants, handworkers, nurses and midwives, teachers, landowners, authors, religious leaders, actresses, printers.

340 Flynn, Elizabeth Gurley. *The Rebel Girl: An Autobiography, My First Life (1906–1929).* 1955. Reprint. New York: International Publishers, 1973. 357 p., pb.
The engaging and informative story of the early political activities of a famous labor leader and socialist. Includes her experiences growing up in poverty around the turn of the century, her growing commitment to socialism, her activity as an Industrial Workers of the World agitator, her relationships with people and causes (Tom Mooney, Sacco and Vanzetti, Joe Hill, strikes, and free speech). Important firsthand account of this period in American history, with a constant thread of feminist thought and activity. Originally published as *I Speak My Own Piece.*

341 Gregory, Chester W. *Women in Defense Work during World War II: An Analysis of the Labor Problem and Women's Rights.* Hicksville, N.Y.: Exposition Press, 1974. 243 p.
A collection of factual material concerning women workers during World War II. Approaches the subject with the attitude that some work is more " suitable" for women, and concludes that "women are available as a reserve labor supply." Includes material on policy-making, recruitment and training programs, problems, specific industries (aircraft, shipbuilding, steel, ammunition, agriculture, and railroads), black women; also includes a comparison of men

and women and a sketchy, inaccurate Equal Rights Amendment chapter. Not very useful; generally refers to workers as "girls."

342 Henry, Alice. *The Trade Union Woman.* New York: D. Appleton, 1915. 314 p.
A classic study of trade unionism and working women. Information on early unions, the Knights of Labor, the Women's Trade Union League, strikes, immigrant women, organizers, vocations and vocational training, marriage, voting, and trade union ideals and policies.

343 Henry, Alice. *Women and the Labor Movement.* New York: George H. Doran, 1923. 241 p.
This historical presentation on working women covers "primitive" and colonial women, machine industry, "women in some modern trade unions," the Women's Trade Union League (of which A. Henry was secretary), legislation, minimum wage, Women's Bureau, World War I, black women, International Federation of Working Women.

344 Hewitt, Margaret. *Wives and Mothers in Victorian Industry.* London: Rockliff, 1958. 245 p.
A description of the effect of industry on women, especially those who worked a double day, and children in the home.

345 Hourwich, Andria Taylor, and Gladys L. Palmer. *I Am a Woman Worker: A Scrapbook of Autobiographies.* 1936. Reprint. New York: Arno Press, 1974. 152 p.
Workers' accounts of their experiences in getting a job, in daily factory work, with open shops and company unions, with trade unions and organized shops, and on strike. The contributors, participants in the Affiliated Schools for Workers, are particularly aware of poor working conditions and the benefits of union organizing.

346 Josephson, Hannah. *The Golden Threads: New England's Mill Girls and Magnates.* 1949. Reprint. New York: Russell and Russell, 1967. 325 p.
A history of the development of the textile industry in America, with emphasis on describing the workers, their working and living conditions, the mill owners, and the conflict between them over ten-hour working days.

347 *Labor History* 17, no. 1 (Winter 1976).
A special issue on women in labor history. Articles are "Organizing the Unorganizable: Three Jewish Women and Their Union," A. Kessler-Harris; "Technology and Women's Work: The Lives of Working Class Women in Pittsburgh, 1870—1900," S. J. Kleinberg; and "Why Women Work: A Comparison of Various Groups in Philadelphia, 1910–1930," B. Klaezynska. Includes documents.

348 Neff, Wanda F. *Victorian Working Women: An Historical and Literary Study of Women in British Industries and Professions 1832–1850.* 1929. Reprint. New York: Humanities Press, 1966. 288 p.
Within a general framework of describing working conditions, Neff presents examples from contemporary literature that deal with textile and other industrial workers, dressmakers, governesses, and "idle" women. A thorough and scholarly book.

349 O'Neill, William L., ed. *Women at Work: Including the Long Day, the Story of a New York Working Girl by Dorothy Richardson (1905); and Inside the New York Telephone Company, by Elinor Langer (1970).* New York: Quadrangle/New York Times, 1972. 360 p., pb.
Two widely read studies of working women. The introductory essay by W. O'Neill discusses the changes in and similarities of women's work in the two periods. The bulk of the book is comprised of the experiences of D. Richardson, a middle-class woman at the turn of the century faced with the necessity of working at unskilled jobs. E. Langer reports on her job experience, including the training period, and describes the internal structure of the telephone company.

350 Pinchbeck, Ivy. *Women Workers and the Industrial Revolution 1750–1850.* 1930. Reprint. New York: Augustus M. Kelley, 1969. 331 p.
Detailed description of British women's work in industry, agriculture, and trade prior to the Industrial Revolution, and "subsequent developments [in] their employment and economic position" (p. 4). Conclusion that these changes led to the increasing financial dependence of married women on their (wage-earning) husbands is true in other societies as well, although Pinchbeck tends to see this dependency as an advance for the art of childrearing and homemaking. Single women gained economic independence during this period.

351 Smuts, Robert W. *Women and Work in America.* 1959. Reprint. New York: Schocken Books, 1971. 155 p., pb.
A clearly written, comprehensive historical review of the changing role of women and work in America, 1890 to 1950. Includes a wealth of information on wages, working conditions, and attitudes toward work and working women.

352 Van Vorst, Mrs. John, and Marie Van Vorst. *The Woman Who Toils: Being the Experience of Two Ladies as Factory Girls.* 1903. Reprint. Los Angeles: University of California, Institute of Industrial Relations, 1974. 163 p., pb.
The report of two women who worked at a variety of factory jobs to publicize the condition of "factory girls." Although not scholarly, provides a description of their experiences. There is little mention of unionization. A useful and informative introduction by Daniel B. Mitchell includes some statistics.

353 Walton, Ronald G. *Women in Social Work.* London: Routledge and Kegan Paul, 1975. 308 p.
A scholarly history of the position of women in social work in England (1860–1971). The material is organized around three themes: social status of women and the struggle for women's rights, women in various spheres of employment, and women's contributions to the development of social work. Concludes that "a new and vital fusion of male and female qualities" is needed for the continued progress of social work.

354 Wertheimer, Barbara Mayer. *We Were There: The Story of Working Women in America.* New York: Pantheon Books, 1977. 427 p., pb.
An important contribution to American women's history. After a prologue on Native American women, the author presents a chronological history including attention to prerevolutionary times, slave women, the transition to factory work, labor unions, white-collar jobs, women in the West, the trade union movement of 1900 to 1914 (the National Women's Trade Union League, garment workers, mill and mine workers, Industrial Workers of the World at Lawrence, Massachusetts). A brief epilogue discusses Coalition of Labor Union Women. Includes eighteen page annotated bibliography.

355 *Women at Work: Ontario 1850–1930.* Toronto: Canadian Women's Educational Press, 1974. 405 p., pb.
"Working within a Marxist framework, the authors have attempted to demonstrate the interrelations between economic and social factors in the secondary position of the woman worker" (Introduction). Includes sections on prostitutes, domestic servants, nurses, teachers, union organizers, and reformers. The chapters are often descriptive rather than analytic. However, this book is of interest because it presents little-known Canadian material and because the authors have tried to work as a collective, a process discussed in the preface.

Psychology

Introduction

In this section those texts of importance to women from the field of psychology are presented. The sources are grouped by subject: General, Sex Differences, Female Personality and Sexuality, and Psychology of Women in Psychoanalytic Theory. Included in the General subsection are those books that present overviews of theories and approaches to the psychology of women and are designed for use as undergraduate texts, and those that address issues cursorily dealt with elsewhere: nonpsychoanalytic psychotherapy, achievement motivation, psychobiological health care, androgyny, and lesbianism.

The works in Sex Differences focus on the definition of biological and psychological differences between the sexes. Some of the books analyze the development of sex differences in the formation of sexual identity. Both social learning and personality theories are represented here. Sex differences research, because of its complexity and great potential for misinterpretation, is occasionally misemployed in its presentation as evidence for hypotheses of sex-role origins.

Texts in Female Personality and Sexuality focus variously on the development of sexuality in personality theory, the effects of biology on psychology and behavior, and aspects of female sexual behavior. Homosexuality, with an emphasis on sexual (versus social) aspects, is dealt with in this section.

The large number of psychoanalytic texts on women warrant a separate section. Included are both classic and modern interpretations of women by psychoanalysts. Psychoanalysis has come under attack by many feminists for theoretical constructs such as penis envy. It is important for those recognizing the value of psychoanalytic theory in the psychology of women to be aware of the many both recent and older texts that substantially build upon the sparse foundations of theory laid down by Freud. Most of these texts offer radically different psychoanalytic approaches to the psychology of women.

General

356   Broderick, Carlfred, and Jessie Bernard. *The Individual, Sex and Society.* Baltimore: Johns Hopkins Press, 1969. 373 p.
Articles geared to aiding teachers of sex education. Part one discusses general issues. Part two examines sexuality in a social-cultural context: premarital sex, definitions of masculinity and femininity. Part three provides three articles that acquaint the teacher with basic information on human sexuality. Part four presents articles on sexual abnormalities, masturbation, homosexuality, and sexual problems. Useful as text for teachers of sex education.

357   Chesler, Phyllis. *Women and Madness.* New York: Avon Books, 1972. 359 p., pb.
An examination of women and psychotherapy in the U.S. Views female "insanity" as unwillingness to submit to stereotypic female role or as overinvolvement with that role. States that a main problem is lack of maternal love in childhood. Unhappiness and frustration from this deprivation are manifested in depression, frigidity, lesbianism—those states defined by psychotherapists as "mental illness." Chesler concludes that present day therapy is harmful to women. Provides lengthy descriptions of women in asylums. Important work.

358   Cox, Sue. *Female Psychology: The Emerging Self.* Chicago: Science Research Associates, 1976. 438 p., pb.
Thirty-three articles prepared for an undergraduate course on the psychology of women. Collection emphasizes direct relationship between political feminism

and female psychology. Explores "societal, interpersonal and psychic levels" of female oppression. Areas covered include biological perspectives, psychological sex differences, cross-cultural variation, ethnic diversity of experience, sexuality, and psychotherapy. Contributions by H. Hacker, E. Maccoby and C. Jacklin, A. Nieto-Gomez, A. Oakley, A. Koedt, M. J. Sherfey, B. Whiting and C. Edwards, M. Mednick, J. Freeman, N. Weisstein, M. Mead, P. Webster, P. Chesler, J. Sawyer. Good collection for undergraduates.

359 Deaux, Kay. *The Behavior of Women and Men.* Belmont, Calif.: Brooks/Cole, 1976. 168 p.
From a social-psychological perspective this book examines the behavior of men and women in a "variety of situations," situation being critical in determination of behavior. Author goes beyond mere documentation of specific sex differences by exploring the situational correlates of sex differences. Book discusses stereotypes, self-evaluation, achievement orientations, interpersonal interaction of men and women, and masculinity, femininity, and androgyny. Through critical assessment of relevant studies, author concludes that significant differences do not lie in "potential" of men and women but rather in "performance" of behavior; when provoked, women and men display equivalent aggression; "fear of success" in women is largely dependent on role expectations of particular situation; men and women are capable of similar degrees of "aggressive, helpful, cooperative and competitive behavior," but situation and stereotype expectations will affect particular *form* these expressions take. Book offers new insights and approaches to study of sex differences. Highly appropriate for use as undergraduate text.

360 Donelson, Elaine, and Jeanne Gullahorn. *Women: A Psychological Perspective.* New York: John Wiley and Sons, 1977. 283 p., pb.
An undergraduate text that explores many facets of the psychology of women. Foci are "psycho-biological" bases of "sex-typed" behavior—including animal studies, biology, sex differences in development; social influences on behavior—including achievement, relationship with mother, friendship; sex roles and androgyny—including professional women, sex roles and social structure, the single woman, and "woman in the family" (p. vii). Presentation is clear. Very useful at undergraduate level.

361 Farber, Seymour, and Roger Wilson. *Man and Civilization: The Potential of Woman.* New York: McGraw-Hill, 1963. 305 p.
Twenty-two symposium papers on the topics of biological versus cultural factors in women's behavioral potential, women's participation in the arts and position in U.S. Includes essays by E. Maccoby, J. Money, and P. Jay. Articles generally outdated. Many overt sexist references.

362 Franks, Violet, and Vasanti Burtle, eds. *Women in Therapy: New Psychotherapies for a Changing Society.* New York: Brunner/Mazel, 1974. 435 p.

Eighteen scholarly articles by therapists on the relationship between middle-class white women and psychotherapy in the U.S. General theme is that psychotherapy has been male dominated and oriented, limiting its positive and emphasizing its negative value for women. In addition, gender role and societal values have significantly affected emotional problems of women. Explores impact of negative stereotype of women on therapist's relationship with patient, common definitions of mental "problems," and various treatments. Critically evaluates various therapeutic methods (e.g., psychoanalysis, Gestalt). Offers suggestions for change in definition and treatment of women's emotional difficulties, emphasizing social-cultural factors. Good collection.

363   Hammer, Signe. *Daughters and Mothers: Mothers and Daughters.* New York: New York Times Book Reviews, 1975. 175 p.
A view of the mother-daughter relationship, based on seventy-five interviews with mothers and daughters. Material consists of personal accounts, with some psychological analyses. Mother-daughter physical-biological and personal relationships and roles are examined. Significant aspects of roles contribute to "gender identity," "personal identity," or "sexual identity" of women.

364   Hyde, Janet, and B. G. Rosenberg. *Half the Human Experience: The Psychology of Women.* Lexington, Mass.: D. C. Heath, 1976. 278 p., pb.
An examination of significant components of a "psychology of women," geared for undergraduates. Clearly and thoroughly presented material on the following topics: definition of goals and reasons for research; mythological and historical concepts of femininity; psychoanalytic, social learning, and cognitive-developmental theories of development; stages in personality development; achievement motivations and abilities; biological factors; sexuality; lesbianism; animal behavior; black women; cross-cultural findings; prospects for relations between the sexes; the interaction between individual's psychology and culture. Calls for changes in institutional and personal psychology, and for "greater valuation attached to female role" (p. 278). Incorporates many significant theories and studies.

365   *Journal of Social Issues* 28, no. 2 (1972). "New Perspectives on Women." 250 p.
Articles edited by M. T. S. Mednick and S. S. Tangri that discuss personality theory, careers, women's image, female playwrights in German literature, sex-role stereotypes, sex-role attitudes and psychological well-being, sex-role attitudes in Finland, maternity and fertility in urban Latin America, childhood experiences, achievement-related conflicts, occupational role innovation among college women, the decision to study medicine, women as politicians, and emancipation of humans. Wide ranging and scholarly.

366   Kaplan, Alexandra, and Joan P. Bean, eds. *Beyond Sex-Role Stereotypes: Readings toward a Psychology of Androgyny.* Boston: Little, Brown, 1976. 392 p., pb.

Twenty-five scholarly articles that critically assess traditional concepts of, and present new perspectives on, sociopsychology of sex roles. Articles arranged into "traditional" and "alternative" studies and their consequences; biological, sexual, and sociocultural factors in the development of sex roles (p. xii). Theme of book is that "by transcending our present limiting sex roles" we can open the way to personal growth (p. 8). Important contribution to theory development. Good collection. Supplementary readings provided.

367 Lasky, Ella, ed. *Humanness: An Exploration into the Mythologies about Women and Men.* New York: MSS Information Corporation, 1975. 543 p.
Forty-three readings prepared for an undergraduate course on sex roles. Takes view that existing sex-role stereotypes oppress both men and women. Articles and essays arranged by topic: psychological consequences of sex-role stereotypes, development of sexual identity in childhood and adolescence, sexuality, sexual abuse, prostitution, marriage and family, childbirth, black and Latin women, men, aging, and mental health. Includes works by J. Freeman, R. Rohrlich-Leavitt, M. Komarovsky, J. Bernard, A. H. Maslow, M. Horner, E. Douvan, T. Colley, I. Broverman. Two reviews of the literature on Latin women, by A. Pescatello, and on male sex role, by J. Pleck. Good collection. Scholarly, readable, and appropriate for undergraduates.

368 Lederer, Wolfgang. *The Fear of Women.* New York: Grune and Stratton, 1968. 286 p.
A nonscientific historical documentation of men's repressed contempt for and fear of women. Lederer draws on myths, art work, psychoanalytic texts to provide evidence of men's distrust of women. Explores male infatuation with female breasts, men's potential contamination from menstruation, "vagina dentata," and male impotency. Limited use.

369 Mednick, Martha T. S.; Sandra S. Tangri; and Lois W. Hoffman; eds. *Women and Achievement: Social and Motivational Analyses.* New York: John Wiley and Sons, 1975. 447 p.
Twenty-five articles that cover sex roles and social change; personality theory and research; sex-role stereotypes; cross-cultural study of marital, educational, and occupational options; sex roles in Sweden, Finland, and the USSR; sex-role inertia on the Kibbutz; working women, education, and fertility; childhood experiences; expectations for success and failure; fear of success; psychological sex differences; sex-labeling of jobs; students; career women's changing self-image. This wide-ranging and scholarly anthology presents much of the most recent material by well-known researchers on these topics. Includes author and subject indexes.

370 Miller, Jean Baker. *Toward a New Psychology of Women.* Boston: Beacon Press, 1976. 135 p., pb.

The psychology of women and their oppression, studied from a perspective that acknowledges their special intimacy with the oppressor (p. 1). Women have developed various strengths in order to deal with domination. Miller explores the psychology of dominance and subordination, inequality, conflict; and adaptive strategies: cooperation, passivity, service to others. Final section examines self-determination and creativity as ways of managing the harmful effects of domination and inequality. Analysis incorporates vignettes. Author interprets women's behavior as positive rather than negative adaptation. Significant contribution.

371 Richardson, Stephen A., and Alan Guttmacher, eds. *Childbearing: Its Social and Psychological Aspects.* Baltimore: Williams and Wilkins, 1967. 245 p.
A social scientific analysis of reproduction. Five articles, by E. Grimm, E. Greenberg, R. Illsley, M. Mead, and N. Newton, variously discuss psychological stress, social class, cross-cultural differences, values, animal behavior, and government policy as factors in childbearing. Authors review and critically evaluate relevant literature, discuss research methods, and suggest areas of research. Thorough and scientific. Valuable work.

372 Rush, Anne Kent. *Getting Clear: Body Work for Women.* New York: Random House, 1973. 286 p., pb.
A book devoted to biopsychological health care for women. Provides exercises and advice on food, exercise, medical care, and psychotherapy. Discusses dynamics of interpersonal relations. Emphasis is on Gestalt therapy. Informative.

373 Unger, Rhoda Kesler, and Florence L. Denmark, eds. *Woman: Dependent or Independent Variable?* New York: Psychological Dimensions, 1975. 828 p.
The goal of this book is "to aid in the definition of a new field of study—the psychology of women" (preface). Articles arranged by topic: sex-role stereotypes, therapists' views of women, development of sex differences and sex roles, sex differences in cognitive functions, concept of psychosexual neutrality, menstruation and pregnancy (the unique female condition), and the internal and external barriers to female achievement. Some articles are followed by suggested paper topics and projects, and most have introductory comments by the editors. Includes a glossary of psychological terminology.

374 Weitz, Shirley. *Sex Roles: Biological, Psychological, and Social Foundations.* New York: Oxford University Press, 1977. 283 p.
An interdisciplinary discussion of sex roles (both female and male, "since they operate as a system"), primarily from a social-psychological perspective (p. 7). In the biology section, aggression, sexuality, psychosexual abnormalities are discussed; the psychology section deals with sex-role socialization, particularly parental agents, school environments and peer groups, and the effects of these

on cognitive ability and socioemotional traits. "Social foundations" includes the family (marriage, sexual division of labor, career choice) and symbolism (sexual pollution, witchcraft, themes in myth and ritual, language, literature, and the arts). The final chapter, "Sex Role Change Through Space and Time," includes information on China, Israel, and Sweden, as well as historical changes in American feminism. A well-organized, informative, and provocative contribution.

375 Williams, Elizabeth. *Notes of a Feminist Therapist.* New York: Praeger, 1976. 183 p.
An analysis of women's problems with loneliness, love, sex, motherhood, depression, and work from a feminist perspective. In second half women's "problems" are redefined. Thesis is that biological, social, "characterological" factors all interact in formation of individual behavior. Williams disagrees with "those who assert that men cause all women's problems or that it is society's negative and discriminatory attitudes that cause them to 'need' therapy" (p. xi).

376 Williams, Juanita. *Psychology of Women: Behavior in a Biosocial Context.* New York: W. W. Norton, 1977. 405 p.
An analysis of significant biological and behavioral factors in the psychology of women. Based on the concept that "human behavior emerges from the neonatal repertoire and becomes organized in a social context" (p. 382). Williams presents knowledgeable and succinct evaluations of Freud, H. Deutsch, E. Erikson, A. Adler, K. Horney, C. Thompson, and M. Mead and their contributions to the study of women. In addition, biological sex differentiation, menstruation, hormones, and the development of physiology and cognition are thoroughly examined. Explores social learning theories of sexual identity. Other sections critically present material on sexuality, birth control, pregnancy, childbirth, and aging. Women and mental illness, prisons, and lifestyles are also discussed. This work is monumental in its thorough presentation and critical evaluation of material on psychology of women. Most outstanding sections are those on biological factors and psychoanalytic theories; weakest, on social analysis. Good bibliography. Extremely useful for introductory course.

377 Wiseman, Jacqueline. *The Social Psychology of Sex.* New York: Harper and Row, 1976. 385 p.
A discussion of the interaction between the sexes from a social-psychological, symbolic-interactionist perspective. Includes twenty-nine articles on general topics: strategies of acquaintance between men and women, components of heterosexual and homosexual relationships, associations between sex and love, sexual stratification and sex roles, social policy and sexual expression. Clear discussion. Valuable collection.

378 Wortis, Helen, and Clara Rabinowitz, eds. *The Women's Movement: Social and Psychological Perspectives.* New York: John Wiley and Sons, Halsted Press, 1972. 151 p., pb.
Brief articles by behavioral scientists: E. Tobach on evolutionary aspects of human gender, M. J. Pollock on changing roles, Z. S. Klapper on child development texts, R. P. Wortis on the effects of the maternal role, B. Linner on the implications of sexual equality, J. Z. Giele on changes in the family, J. B. Miller and I. Mothner on psychological consequences of sexual inequality, M. Adams on single women, T. T. Walker and C. K. Riessman on recent writings by women in the movement, and M. G. Keiffer and P. A. Warren with a thirty-six page resource bibliography.

Sex Differences

379 Friedman, Richard; Ralph Richart; and Raymond Wiele. *Sex Differences in Behavior.* New York: John Wiley and Sons, 1974. 489 p.
Twenty-four articles on "sexual differences in psychological functioning." Authors variously discuss "influences of psychological, physiological, and social systems on each other within a sex-differences framework" (p. xi). Discussions are based on scientific studies and topics include mother-infant interaction; early childhood experiences; development of sex differences in behavior, gender identity; psychoendrocrine differences; "aggression, adaptation, and evolution." Extremely valuable in the presentation of recent research. Material is very complex.

380 Hutt, Corinne. *Males and Females.* Baltimore: Penguin, 1972. 141 p., pb.
A compilation of data on the "biological basis" of sex differentiation (physiological and psychological). Material on genetic and hormonal differences; sexual development; effects of biological factors on intelligence, aggression, creativity, ambition, values, and sensory acuity. While discussion is scholarly, many of Hutt's findings are not supported by recent research (see Maccoby and Jacklin, 1974 [no. 382]).

381 Maccoby, Eleanor, ed. *The Development of Sex Differences.* Stanford: Stanford University Press, 1966. 351 p., pb.
A collection of five articles on the acquisition of sex differences. Includes effect of sex hormones on behavior (D. Hamburg and D. Lunde), social learning theory (W. Mischel), cognitive development (L. Kholberg), cultural institutions and task differences (R. D'Andrade), sex differences in intellect (E. Maccoby), and a one hundred page annotated bibliography (R. Oetzel). Also contains a summary of sex differences research. Constitutes major work in study of socialization. Useful resource for sex differences research. Moderately complex.

382 Maccoby, Eleanor, and Carol Jacklin. *The Psychology of Sex Differences.* Stanford: Stanford University Press, 1974. 635 p.
A scientific analysis of psychological differences between the sexes based on the examination and incorporation of hundreds of relevant psychological studies. Two main areas of concentration are intellect and achievement (perception, learning, memory), and social behavior (social approach/ avoidance, power relations, "emotionality," and "temperament activity level"). A third section discusses the "origins" of psychological sex differences through exploration of sex-typing and socialization processes. Authors posit that whereas there exist certain "sex-linked biological predispositions," "social shaping" is of great significance in the acquisition of "sex-typed behavior" (p. 275). Book presents much new information on sex differences. Work is framed in scientific excellence and abounds in clarity and precision. Contains a two hundred page annotated bibliography of studies used in analysis. An indispensable resource in study of women.

383 Money, John, and Anke A. Ehrhardt. *Man and Woman, Boy and Girl: Differentiation and Dimorphism of Gender Identity from Conception to Maturity.* Baltimore: Johns Hopkins Press, 1972. 263 p., pb.
A scientific analysis of prenatal sexual differentiation, and its interaction with postnatal behavioral and biological sexual differentiation. Employs scientific studies of hermaphrodites and other sexual "anomalies" to demonstrate that "nature has ordained a major part of [postnatal] human gender identity differentiation" (p. 18). Examines the effects of sex chromosomes on fetal sex development; fetal hormones' effects on the brain and behavior; the cumulative effect of these factors on gender identity and role formation. Money concludes that "everything pertaining . . . to [opposite] gender role is brain coded as negative and unfit for use" (p. 19). Important study.

384 Rosenberg, B. G., and Brian Sutton-Smith. *Sex and Identity.* New York: Holt, Rinehart and Winston, 1972. 91 p., pb.
Presents the fundamental arguments of the biological-social bases of sex-role differentiation in sociology, biology, social learning, psychoanalysis, anthropology, and comparative psychology. Basic theories of each discipline are summarized and examined clearly and succinctly. Authors begin by suggesting that the "categorization of sex role differences [is] a convenient but typological error" (p. 88). They end with the view that the typology is not a "psychometric error or cultural habit" but that "society without sex stereotypes is much less interesting and productive than societies with definitions of sex role behavior" (p. 90). While book's thesis appears simplistic, its summary of major theories has great potential use in classroom.

385 Tavris, Carol, and Carole Offir. *The Longest War: Sex Differences in Perspective.* New York: Harcourt Brace Jovanovich, 1977. 297 p., pb.
An undergraduate text that examines the "alienation" between men and

women in terms of sex differences and social stereotypes (p. 4). Provides brief historical review of sexual inequality, sex differences in ability, personality, and sexuality; theories on sex differences from biological, psychoanalytic, social learning, sociological, and evolutionary perspectives are presented. Discussion is clear and enjoyable, but lacks sufficiently thorough analysis of many points.

386   Teitelbaum, Michael. *Sex Differences: Social and Biological Perspectives.* New York: Doubleday, Anchor, 1976. 224 p., pb.
Six articles by specialists on primate behavior (J. Lancaster), cross-cultural variation (J. Brown), biology (A. Barfield), and socialization (V. Stewart) combined in a general examination of sex differences. Thesis is that "sex is both a social and biological characteristic" (p. 18). Articles successfully integrate the two concepts in a clear, concise framework. Generalizations are absent. While articles posit some controversial conclusions (i.e., natural constraint of children on women), book is scholarly and presents good overview of sex differences. Useful in introductory, interdisciplinary courses.

387   Terman, Lewis, and Catharine Cox Miles. *Sex and Personality: Studies in Masculinity and Femininity.* 1936. Reprint. New York: Russell and Russell, 1968. 589 p.
An important pioneer effort in delineation of behavioral differences between the sexes. Based on eleven years of research, the study attempts not a definition of origins (biological versus social) of sex differences but establishment of the validity of assumptions about the behavioral differences between the sexes. Findings are that sex differences are largely dependent on "schooling, age, occupation, interests, and domestic milieu" (p. 463). Parental influence is also significant. Study has been superseded, but represents important work. Limited use in classroom.

388   Yorburg, Betty. *Sexual Identity.* New York: John Wiley and Sons, 1974. 153 p.
Examination of sex roles. Discusses biological evidence for sex-role differentiation but insufficiently surveys psychological contributions to study. Analyzes women in hunting/gathering and nonindustrial societies. Summarizes female role in "modern societies": Middle East, Sweden, China, Japan, Latin America, USSR, and U.S. Demonstrates cursory understanding of anthropology and history.

Female Personality and Sexuality

389   Bardwick, Judith. *Psychology of Women: A Study of Bio-Cultural Conflicts.* New York: Harper and Row, 1971. 219 p., pb.
An analysis of the biosocial life crises of women (childhood, puberty, pregnancy) based on the assumption that hormone differences between males

and females determine behavioral differences. Describes as some "natural tendencies": greater aggression, independence, and early genital arousal of men contrasted with greater passivity, dependence, lesser achievement motivation of women. Bardwick calls for increased cultural valuation of feminine qualities, and emphasis on combined qualities of masculinity and femininity in the ideal personality. Distinction between biological and cultural bases of behavior is often obscured in analysis. Good bibliography.

390   Bardwick, Judith; Elizabeth Douvan; Matina S. Horner; and David Gutman. *Feminine Personality and Conflict.* Belmont, Calif.: Wadsworth Publishing, Brooks/Cole, 1970. 97 p., pb.
Four articles, one by each of the authors. Bardwick analyzes the psychic conflict resulting from women's ambivalence toward menstruation, pregnancy, childbirth, lactation, and menopause. Women express conflict about "sexual use of their bodies" through "somatic symptoms in the reproductive system," and in "premenstrual feelings of anxiety, hostility, depression, and inadequacy" (p. 3). Douvan explores conflicts that confront adolescent girls. Girls' problems derive from both "biologically induced conflicts" and the imposition of "narrowly conceived (cultural) sex role expectations" (pp. 41–42). M. Horner analyzes "fear of success" syndrome characteristic of U.S. women. Gutman analyzes "autocentric" ego style found among women, Native American men, and "hippie" males in contrast to the "allocentric" ("successful adaptation") ego style of white males (p. 79). While some concepts are unsupported by recent studies, this collection is basic.

391   Bardwick, Judith, ed. *Readings on the Psychology of Women.* New York: Harper and Row, 1972. 324 p., pb.
Forty-four articles by social scientists on socialization, psychobiological development, sexual development, psychological effects of traditional female roles on women, and analysis of the feminist movement. Specific topics include mother-infant interaction; sex differences in intellect and prenatal development; women and depression, divorce, pregnancy, and the professions. Incorporates material on Soviet, Israeli, and Chinese women. Valuable collection. Basic text.

392   Beach, Frank, ed. *Sex and Behavior.* New York: John Wiley and Sons, 1965. 570 p.
Twenty-one scientific articles on human and animal sexual behavior. Topics include sexual behavior in mice, canaries, rhesus monkeys (H. Harlow), baboons (I. De Vore), cats, and doves; evolutionary factors in sexuality (E. Caspari); hormones (J. de Groot); genetics; psychosexual orientation, gender role, sexual patterns in a Pacific society (W. Davenport); effects of household structure and "situational factors" (P. Gebhard) on sexual behavior; sexual response in men and women (W. Masters and V. Johnson), and "stimuli" affecting sexual behavior. Scholarly collection. Basic text.

393 Boston Women's Health Book Collective. *Our Bodies, Ourselves.* New York: Simon and Schuster, 1971. 271 p., pb.
Provides valuable information on women's physiology, sexuality, and health care. Clear, illustrated discussions of anatomy, menstruation, childbirth, and pregnancy; masturbation, virginity; heterosexual and homosexual relationships, celibacy; birth control, rape, venereal disease, abortion; childbearing and menopause. Discusses lesbianism and health care for women. Readable.

394 Eysenck, A. J. *Sex and Personality.* Austin: University of Texas Press, 1976. 220 p.
A study of the interaction between personality and sexual attitudes and behaviors. From analysis of samples of male and female adults, students, and psychiatric patients, Eysenck concludes that there is a distinct correlation between libido, personality, and sexual behavior. Finds that age and social class are important variables in formation of attitudes. States that "attitudes and behavior discussed . . . as well as personality traits associated with them, have a clear genetic basis" in the sex hormones of androgen and estrogen (p. 225). High level of complexity.

395 Ford, Clellan S., and Frank Beach. *Patterns of Sexual Behavior.* New York: Harper and Row, 1951. 268 p.
An important attempt to delineate the evolutionary, physiological, and culturally universal components of human sexual behavior. Scientifically compares primate and human physiological and behavioral aspects of sexuality to determine evolutionary/hereditary factors. Explores ethnographic data from HRAF in defining common features of sexual behavior. Examines physiological characteristics of human sexual response. This significant work dispels many pre-1951 misconceptions about sexuality.

396 Gebhard, Paul; Jan Raboch; and Hans Giese. *The Sexuality of Women.* London: Andre Deutsch, 1970. 133 p.
Three articles on different aspects of female sexuality. Gebhard presents a clear and thorough summary of data on animal and human sexuality (childhood, orgasms, intercourse, homosexuality), emphasizing female sexuality, physiology, and behavior. Raboch analyzes women's difficulties in experiencing sexual satisfaction and concludes that these result from physiological malfunctions and problems in family background. Giese incorporates psychoanalytic case histories and studies on female sexuality in an analysis of narcissism, homosexuality, orgasm, and "passivity." Gebhard's article provides valuable review of literature.

397 Goldman, George D., and Donald Milman. *Modern Woman: Her Psychology and Sexuality.* Springfield, Ill.: Charles C. Thomas, 1969. 273 p.
Nine scholarly articles on the sexual psychology of women. Includes a review of the literature on female sexuality (S. Waxenberg), "Fear of Loving" (E.

Fried), sex role and personality (S. Guber), body image (H. Guze), childbearing (E. Grimm), frigidity (L. Schaefer), depression (R. Spiegel), promiscuity (M. Bergman), and homosexuality (R. Eisenbud). Important work although some concepts are outdated.

398 Hammer, Signe, ed. *Women: Body and Culture.* New York: Harper and Row, 1975. 337 p., pb.
Twenty-three articles by acclaimed psychologists, psychoanalysts, anthropologists, and sex researchers on the interaction of female sexuality and culture. Hammer posits that sexuality is "perhaps the deepest level" of identity formation (p. 8). Articles divided by topic: sexuality; masturbation, sexual identity, and orgasm; menstruation and menopause; pregnancy, childbirth, and childcare. Articles by K. Horney, J. Money, H. Deutsch, W. Masters and V. Johnson, C. Thompson, A. Kinsey, and M. J. Sherfey. Introductions to sections summarize contents succinctly and clearly. Good collection.

399 Kinsey, Alfred; Wardell B. Pomeroy; Clyde Martin; and Paul Gebhard. *Sexual Behavior in the Human Female.* Philadelphia: W. B. Saunders, 1953. 763 p.
A monumental study, based on fifteen years' research, of the sexual behavior of 5,940 white females. Goal of work is to "discover what people do sexually, what factors may account for their pattern of sexual behavior, how their sexual experiences have affected their lives, and what social significance there may be in each type of behavior" (p. 3). Essentially a statistical analysis of the relationship between variables such as age and marital status, and sexual activity. Discusses sexual behaviors (masturbation, coitus) and compares this with data on male sexual activity. An early but important contribution; superseded by Masters and Johnson. Much detail. Excellent bibliography.

400 Money, John, ed. *Sex Research: New Developments.* New York: Holt, Rinehart and Winston, 1965. 219 p.
Eleven classic articles on female sexuality. Includes W. Masters and V. Johnson—sexual response in women; Money—psychosexual differentiation, concluding that effects of hormones on behavior are presently unclear; H. F. Harlow and M. K. Harlow—isolation of rhesus monkeys and the importance of contact with other monkeys for social development; C. H. Phoneux—demonstration of hormones' effects on prenatal genital tract differentiation and "sex-related behavior" of monkeys. Valuable collection.

401 Money, John, and Patricia Tucker. *Sexual Signatures: On Being a Man or a Woman.* Boston: Little, Brown, 1975. 250 p.
A readable summary for undergraduates of Money's research on sexuality. Authors detail sexual development in the prenatal stage, infancy and early childhood, later childhood, adolescence, and maturity. Includes discussion of sex hormones and the brain, and gender identity. Stresses the wide spectrum and the mutability of sexuality outside the reproductive functions of

impregnation, childbirth, lactation, and menstruation. Useful text on sexuality.

402 Saghir, Marcel T., and Robins, Eli. *Male and Female Homosexuality: A Comprehensive Investigation.* Baltimore: Williams and Wilkins, 1973. 341 p.
A detailed scientific study that compares male and female homosexuals to male and female heterosexuals and to each other. Nonhospitalized homosexual volunteers (104 men, 61 women) were contrasted in childhood development, sexual "psychologic responses" (attachments, fantasies, etc.), degree of psychopathology (neurosis, psychosis, etc.), parental influences and family life, homosexual and heterosexual practices, and "sociologic" characteristics (delinquency, religion, socioeconomic status, etc.) to 87 men and 44 women manifesting predominantly heterosexual behavior. Study concentrates on description of homosexual behavior as opposed to delineation of etiology of homosexuality. Among numerous findings that refute traditional assumptions: psychopathology exhibited is not significantly greater for homosexual than for heterosexual men and women; same-sex siblings are important in development of homosexuality; homosexuality does not usually stem from either sexual trauma with opposite sex in childhood or from fear of heterosexual attachments; homosexuality develops early in childhood and adolescence with a concomitant display of "cross-gender symptomatic behavior [and] developing psychologic responses" (p. 262); the greater family and parental conflicts in homosexual childhood could be due to negative response of parents to developing homosexuality in child; sociologically, homosexual men and women are more like their heterosexual counterparts than each other. Book is major contribution to study of homosexuality. Scientifically invalidates most studies suggesting "a priori" sickness of homosexuals (p. 317).

403 Schaeffer, Dirk L. *Sex Differences in Personality: Readings.* Belmont, Calif.: Brooks/Cole, 1971. 186 p., pb.
Seventeen articles that either present recent research or analyze traditional theory in sex differences and personality. Section one explores attitudes, perceptions of each sex about themselves and members of opposite sex. Social learning (J. Kagan, D. Lynn) and Freudian theories (Freud, G. Blum) are presented together with P. Goldberg's research on women's "prejudice" against other women. Part two describes not easily observable differences in behavior: dreams (A. Paolino), memorization (W. Kaess), "play configuration" (E. Erikson), and cognition (D. Schaeffer, J. Eisenberg). Last section analyzes differences between the sexes in sexual behavior. J. Barmack criticizes Kinsey's work, N. Lehrman presents excerpts from an interview with W. Masters and V. Johnson, and others present new research. In his extensive abstracts, in which articles' theses are critically assessed and placed in temporal and theoretical context, Schaeffer emphasizes the importance of identifying the relevance/significance of sex differences, not merely their existence. Book offers many new approaches to study of sex differences in personality.

404   Seaman, Barbara, and Gideon Seaman, M.D. *Women and the Crisis in Sex Hormones.* New York: Rawson Associates, 1977. 502 p.
A detailed, readable examination of birth control, menopause, and the use of hormones. The medical history and public response to DES, ERT, and the pill are examined in depth. Birth control methods, including the pill, organic methods, and male contraceptives, are thoroughly investigated. Use of sex hormones in treatment of menopausal symptoms and in development of male and female athletes is evaluated. Authors promote use of diaphragm and provide wealth of information on organic treatment of menopausal symptoms, in overall advocacy of women's control over their bodies. Book is excellent guide to, and presents much recent information on, all areas noted.

405   Sherfey, Mary Jane. *The Nature and Evolution of Female Sexuality.* New York: Random House, 1966. 146 p., pb.
One of the first major works on female sexuality and behavior. Based on her analysis of data from W. Masters and V. Johnson, Sherfey refutes the notion that clitoral orgasm represents an infantile response and is distinct from "mature" vaginal orgasm, and provides evidence supporting Masters and Johnson's conclusion that the clitoris (instead of the vagina) is the focus of female orgasmic activity. Lengthy description of female sexual functioning. Classic study.

406   Sherman, Julia. *On The Psychology of Women: A Survey of Empirical Studies.* Springfield, Ill.: Charles C. Thomas, 1971. 238 p.
A scientific analysis of psychological sex differences. Covers differential prenatal development and acquisition of hormones; psychological differences in childhood, adolescence, and adulthood. Sherman concludes that there are sex differences in ability to complete spatial tasks, sex drive, physical strength, verbal facility, and aggression. Discusses socialization, Oedipal complex, and "bio-behavioral" effects of menstruation and pregnancy. Some conclusions not supported by E. Maccoby and C. Jacklin, 1974 (no. 382). Contains good bibliography.

407   Stoller, Robert. *Sex and Gender: Volume I, The Development of Masculinity and Femininity.* 1968. Reprint. New York: Jason Aronson, 1974. 377 p.
Presentation of Stoller's work on sexuality and gender identity. Based on study of eighty-five patients with abnormal sexual physiology or serious problems of gender identity, Stoller concludes that sex and gender may be "quite independent of each other" (p. viii), but there are "biological forces" that contribute to learning of gender identity (p. xi). In spite of androcentric bias, book constitutes major work, evidenced by documentation of early formation of nonconflictive gender identity.

408   Wagner, Nathaniel. *Perspectives on Human Sexuality: Psychological, Social and Cultural Findings.* New York: Human Sciences Press, 1974. 509 p.
Twenty-six scholarly articles of recent research on sex differences and sexual development, factors in sexual behavior, cross-cultural perspectives on sexual behavior, and specialized studies of sexual behavior. Each article constitutes original research published for the first time. Includes articles by J. Money, P. Goldberg, I. Broverman, L. Rainwater, P. Abramson, R. LeVine, and J. Kanter and M. Zelnick among others. Good collection.

409   Wolff, Charlotte. *Love Between Women.* 1971. Reprint. London: Gerald Duckworth, 1973. 225 p.
A scientific study of lesbians from autobiographies and interviews of 108 lesbians. Wolff sets forth a theory of lesbianism based on inherent bisexuality of women resulting from "retention of a masculine part, the clitoris," the problematic relationship with mother—specifically frustration resulting from inadequate affection and attention, and intense emotionality (p. 48). Wolff states, "Lesbians expect . . . nothing less than wish fulfillment of an incestuous mother-daughter relationship" (p. 87). Wolff emphasizes the flexibility of roles (from object to subject) in lesbian relationships. Study is thought-provoking. Reviews psychological literature on lesbianism.

410   Zubin, Joseph, and John Money. *Contemporary Sexual Behavior: Critical Issues in the 1970s.* Baltimore: Johns Hopkins Press, 1973. 441 p.
Twenty-two scientific articles on recent sex research. Topics include "prenatal hormones and subsequent sexual dimorphism of behavior; brain function and sexual behavior; maternalism and women's sexuality; sex, marital status, and family structure; sex education; and the psychophysiological aspects of the sexual act and treatment of its disturbances" (p. xvii). Good collection.

Psychology of Women in Psychoanalytic Theory

411   Bettelheim, Bruno. *Symbolic Wounds.* Norwich, Eng.: Fletcher and Son, 1955. 267 p., pb.
An anthropological-psychoanalytic theory of male circumcision and subincision based primarily on data on schizophrenic British adolescents and Arunta Australian aboriginal male and female puberty ceremonies. Contrary to traditional theory that states circumcision is based on castration anxiety, Bettelheim posits that male envy of female reproductive organs and processes is motivation for the practice of circumcision and the accompanying ritual. Circumcision provides men with symbolic power. While slightly ethnocentric and psychoanalytically outdated, book presents provocative view.

412   Bonaparte, Marie. *Female Sexuality.* New York: International Universities Press, 1953. 225 p.

A psychobiological analysis of female psychology. Posits that there exists a "far greater frequency of defective adaptation to the purely erotic [versus reproductive] function in woman than in man" (p. 1). "Essential feminine masochism," frigidity, inability to transfer clitoral eroticism to vagina, inability to give up desire for penis, and "masculine affiliation" of the clitoris are associated with the "belated development . . . of the clitoris" (pp. 76, 10). Bonaparte examines libido development in boys and girls, effect of siblings and parents on development of girls' sexuality, and female passivity. An early treatise, constituting a major work in psychoanalytic theory.

413 Chasseguet-Smirnel, Janine. *Female Sexuality: New Psychoanalytic Views.* Ann Arbor: University of Michigan Press, 1970. 213 p.
An excellent collection of six articles that present new psychoanalytic perspectives on female sexuality. Authors agree on the "overwhelming importance of the mother for the personality and later sexual adjustment of the little girl," and emphasize that female psychology cannot be understood solely as a correlate of male psychology (p. vi). Articles include examination of male bias in psychoanalytic theory (C. David); importance of change from maternal to paternal object (C. Lugret-Parat); female narcissism (B. Grunberger); female homosexuality (J. McDougall); penis envy (M. Tovok); female guilt and relationship to father (J. Chasseguet-Smirnel). Significant contribution to theory of female psychology. Extremely valuable.

414 Deutsch, Helene. *The Psychology of Women: A Psychoanalytic Interpretation, Volume One.* New York: Grune and Stratton, 1944. 395 p., pb.
A presentation of Deutsch's theories on the psychology of women. As J. Williams, in *Psychology of Women: Behavior in a Biosocial Context* (no. 376), states, Deutsch traces the psychological development of the women from childhood through adolescence and menstruation. Deutsch describes the qualities of narcissism, eroticism, passivity, and masochism inherent in women, and delineates the female "masculinity complex," homosexuality, and social effects on personality. She views motherhood (a balance of joy, pleasure, and pain) and "receptivity" as constituting normality. Views the active and aggressive woman as in conflict with her environment. Major theses of the book enlarge upon Freudian theory: penis envy is less important than envy which occurs in both boys and girls; Oedipal complex does not end in childhood but continues into adulthood. Deutsch's work is classic in psychoanalytic literature.

415 Deutsch, Helene. *The Psychology of Women: A Psychoanalytic Interpretation, Volume Two, Motherhood.* New York: Grune and Stratton, 1945. 488 p., pb.
An early psychoanalytic study of motherhood, emphasizing the particular personality features of mothers and "the emotional phenomena that seem to be related to the child's helplessness and need for care" (p. 17). Deutsch views motherhood, where the balance of feminine masochism and narcissism is

expressed, as the apex of woman's psychological life. Motherhood also involves intense eroticism and sexuality. Deutsch examines pregnancy, conception, birth, lactation, mother-child relations, and unmarried, adoptive, and stepmothers. Useful in the study of classic psychoanalytic works.

416 Freud, Sigmund. *Sexuality and the Psychology of Love.* Edited by Philip Rieff. New York: Collier, 1963. 220 p., pb.
Sixteen of Freud's papers on sexuality. Includes "Some Psychological Consequences of the Anatomical Distinction between the Sexes," "Female Sexuality," "A Child is Being Beaten," "The Psychogenesis of a Case of Homosexuality in a Woman." Excellent collection, containing Freud's important discussions on women.

417 Freud, Sigmund. *Three Essays on the Theory of Sexuality.* Translated and edited by James Strachey. New York: Basic Books, 1962. 110 p.
Three of Freud's classic essays on sexuality: "The Sexual Aberrations," "Infantile Sexuality" (discussion of penis envy), and "The Transformations of Puberty" (contains section on differential development of males and females). Includes Freud's summary of the essays. Writing is clear, but ideas are very complex.

418 Horney, Karen. *Feminine Psychology.* New York: W. W. Norton, 1967. 245 p.
Fifteen of Horney's most frequently referenced articles, including "Flight From Womanhood." Other topics: frigidity, female masochism, problems of "monogamous ideal" and marriage, "psychogenic factors" in female disorders, and "dread of women." Horney critically examines Freudian theory on women and offers alternative analysis. Posits that penis envy is cultural and based on envy of male domination and power (versus envy of sex organ). Cites male envy of female reproduction. While she supports many traditional Freudian concepts (e.g., that women want to be men), her work constitutes important contribution to psychoanalytic theory on women.

419 Johnson, Robert. *She!: A Contribution to Understanding Feminine Psychology, Based on the Myth of Amor and Psyche, and Using Jungian Psychological Concepts.* King of Prussia, Pa.: Religious Publishing, 1976. 91 p.
An examination of psychological femaleness within the context of the Amor and Psyche myth. Attempts to delineate personality attributes of femininity (anima), and to lesser extent masculinity (animus). While simplistically incorporates some Jungian concepts, material generally lends support to domination of women by men in its analysis. Little use in classroom.

420 Miller, Jean Baker, ed. *Psychoanalysis and Women.* Baltimore: Penguin, 1973. 375 p., pb.
Articles that challenge Freud's traditional conceptions of the female psyche.

Contains classic articles by K. Horney, C. Thompson, A. Adler, F. Fromm-Reichmann, G. Zilboorg, M. J. Sherfey, M. B. Cohen, P. Chodoff, R. Stoller, R. Seidenberg, and others. Authors grouped as "pertinent pioneers," such as K. Horney, and those with "new evidence." Presents views on future perspectives of women. Includes "Flight From Womanhood," "Penis Envy in Women," "Nature of Female Sexuality," and "Bisexuality." A valuable collection of important psychoanalytic theories on women.

421 Mitchell, Juliet. *Psychoanalysis and Feminism.* New York: Random House, 1974. 435 p., pb.
An analysis of women's oppression within a primarily Freudian psychoanalytic framework. Wilhelm Reich's synthesis of Marxism and psychoanalysis, while "offer[ing] little" theoretically, does present some "very pertinent observations" of use to feminists, Mitchell states (p. 202). Despite R. D. Laing's contributions, he insufficiently distinguishes between neurosis and psychosis (he says psychosis is simply a more severe neurosis), and this constitutes a serious deficiency in his argument as he "ignore[s] the importance of the patriarchal culture" (p. 260). Mitchell contends that the universal Oedipal complex, in which boys and girls want to take the father's place, both want to be the phallus for the mother, and in which only boys can succeed, is the universal characteristic of patriarchal societies. She states that in patriarchal society "femininity is in part a repressed condition that can only be secondarily acquired in a distorted form" (p. 404). Mitchell adheres to Freudian concept of penis envy in girls. She calls for an "overthrow of patriarchy" to end the universal oppression of women. Scholarly; extremely complex theory. Important contribution to theory development.

422 Nagera, Humberto. *Female Sexuality and the Oedipus Complex.* New York: Jason Aronson, 1975. 141 p.
A complex theoretical analysis of the development of the Oedipal complex in girls. Nagera sets forth the five developmental stages: 1) change of object from mother to father, 2) "abandonment of the clitoris as the essential erotogenic zone," 3) adoption of a feminine "position," 4) development of "passivity" in place of "activity," 5) development of the ego with a concomitant acceptance of the absence of a penis in women and of the "substitutes" (i.e., babies) for it, the "reduction of penis envy," and adoption of "suitable feminine identification" (pp. 12–13). Nagera thoroughly explains each stage and provides case studies. High level of complexity renders the work somewhat inappropriate for undergraduate course.

423 Reich, Wilhelm. *Sex-Pol: Essays 1929–1934.* Edited by Lee Baxandall. New York: Randon House, Vintage Books, 1972. 378 p., pb.
Reich's six important essays that integrate Marxist and psychoanalytic perspectives. Includes "Dialectical Materialism and Psychoanalyisis" and "The Imposition of Sexual Morality." Specifically, Reich attempts to examine

Marx's "theory of alienation as it applies to the sexual realm" (p. xv). As Baxandall states, Reich believed "capitalism is not only responsible for our beliefs, the ideas of which we are conscious, but also for related unconscious attitudes... spontaneous reactions which proceed from our character structure" (p. xviii). Good collection. Discussion is complex.

424 Ruitenbeck, Hendrik M., ed. *Psychoanalysis and Female Sexuality.* New Haven: College and University Press, 1966. 246 p.
Fifteen articles on female sexuality by psychoanalysts. Topics include cultural versus biological (e.g., penis envy) nature of women's relation to men (C. Thompson); Oedipal complex (E. Jones, J. Lampl-de Groot) and pre-Oedipal stage (Freud) in women; "Denial of the Vagina" (K. Horney); female homosexuality (H. Deutsch), passivity, masochism, and femininity (M. Bonaparte), and "masculinity complex" (Van Ophuijsen); clitoral versus vaginal orgasm (P. Greenacre, J. Marmor, S. Lorand); relation of sexuality to other emotions (e.g., self-concept) (A. H. Maslow, D. Freedman, J. Riviere). Good collection.

425 Stoller, Robert J. *Sex and Gender: Volume II, The Transsexual Experiment.* New York: Jason Aronson, 1975. 298 p.
A primarily psychoanalytic study of transsexualism among men. Posits that transsexualism is similar to the development of masculinity and femininity in that it is an identity in itself and results from nonconflictive (versus conflicting) forces. Stoller cites the inherent bisexuality in men and women, the tendency for boys to be more vulnerable to the formation of weak ego structures, and the strong parental influence in gender formation as critical factors in the development of transsexualism. Important work.

426 Strouse, Jean, ed. *Women and Analysis: Dialogues on Psychoanalytic Views of Femininity.* New York: Grossman, 1974. 367 p., pb.
Essays by Freud, K. Abraham, E. Erikson, C. Jung, K. Horney, and R. Stoller on female psychology, with emphasis on the development of sexuality. Each major work on the topic is followed by a critical analysis by one of the following: J. Mitchell, M. Mead, E. Janeway, J. Kovel, M. Cavell, B. Glepi. A scholarly work that sets forth the important approaches to, and critical analysis of, theories of female sexuality.

427 Thompson, Clara. *On Women.* New York: New American Library, 1964. 185 p., pb.
A presentation of women's psychology in a sociopsychoanalytic framework. Thompson emphasizes "cultural factors [that] explain the tendency of women to feel inferior about their sex," that is, social institutions and the patriarchal system (p. 73). Thompson uses cross-cultural data to refute universality of feminine psychology. Views "body parts" as "symbolic [versus actual]... representation of problems." Analyzes "penis envy as a sign of person's power,"

and women's "attitudes as not qualitatively different from that found in any minority group in a competitive culture" (p. 75). Book is important contribution and very readable. Offers novel approach to psychoanalytic study of women.

428 Ulanov, Ann Belford. *The Feminine in Jungian Psychology and in Christian Theology.* Evanston: Northwestern University Press, 1971. 342 p. An analysis of "the feminine" in Jungian theory and its relation to Christian theology. Feminine is defined as the "hitherto neglected pole in the polarity [masculinity/femininity] of being which is intrinsic to wholeness (p. 15). The psyche is both "empirical and symbolic" and can be understood only in its nonrational terms (versus translation into "rational abstract structures" [c.f. Freud]). The inherent structural polarity of masculine/feminine archetype exists in both men and women, and there exist a collective unconscious and anima/animus. Briefly but clearly reviews Freud, K. Horney, and others, describing their biological (Freud), cultural (K. Horney), instead of symbolic (Jung) perspectives.

Sociology

Introduction

Resources on women from the field of sociology are presented in this section of the *Guide.* The books and special issues of journals are divided according to their principal emphasis: General, Women and Society, Marriage and Motherhood, Sex Roles and Socialization. The General sources offer either a broad analysis of women's roles primarily in U.S. or discussions of issues involved in the study of women, or they are textbooks on the sociology of women. In addition some classic texts and special topics not covered elsewhere are included.

The sources in Women and Society focus on women's confrontation with political, economic, education, religious, and legal systems. Rape and wife beating are also topics dealt with here. Empirical studies (e.g., women in academia, women in prisons) and theoretical analyses consistently point to the obstacles encountered by women in their struggle for equality. The research helps elucidate those factors that contribute to and perpetuate women's subordinate status.

A second area of research is Marriage and Motherhood. These sources include investigations of the family and women's roles as wives and mothers from both feminist and nonfeminist perspectives. New evidence and expanded theoretical perspectives lend increasing support to the thesis that women hold a pivotal position in the household in both decision-making and socialization. Most sources on women's economic roles, including as working wives and mothers, are listed in the Economics section.

A final area of investigation is Sex Roles and Socialization. Sources variously discuss the characteristics of sex roles, biosocial bases of sex roles, relation of sex roles to the social structure, the persistence of stereotypes, and the process of socialization. Increasingly, sociologists are discovering that the elements of gender identity are more subtle and are acquired at an earlier age than previously assumed. Work has begun on identifying the complex and often oppressive components of the male sex role in the U.S. Sources on this topic are evaluated here.

General

429 Andreas, Carol. *Sex and Caste in America.* Englewood Cliffs, N.J.: Prentice-Hall, 1971. 146 p., pb.
This book is designed for high school readers; it is a simplistic, general, and sometimes inaccurate discussion of history, work, socialization, legal issues, and other topics. The use of the term and concept *caste* is not appropriate to America, despite the prefatory explanation.

430 Brown, Donald R., ed. *The Role and Status of Women in the Soviet Union.* New York: Teachers College Press, 1968. 139 p.
Symposium lectures on working mothers, women students, image of women in Soviet Union, changing Soviet family, children, and marriage.

431 Carson, Josephine. *Silent Voices: The Southern Negro Woman Today.* New York: Dell, 1969. 273 p.
An account of Carson's travels through the South and interviews with black women. Some interesting information on women's views on marriage, politics, and their lives. Limited classroom use.

432 Cassara, Beverly Benner, ed. *American Women: Their Changing Image.* Boston: Beacon Press, 1962. 141 p.
A collection of articles on women as professionals, volunteers, teachers of values, industrial workers, educators; now outdated in its emphasis on women's primary roles as wives and mothers.

433 De Souza, Alfred, ed. *Women in Contemporary India: Traditional Images and Changing Roles.* Delhi: Manohar Book Service, 1975. 264 p.
Essays on a variety of topics—employment and family change, etiquette (forms of address), Kerala women, changing self image, the law, religion, aging women, family status and working women, Asian women in Britain, women in International Women's Year. Useful introduction includes summary of findings in each article. Six page bibliography. Most of these articles were previously published in *Social Action* 25 (July–September 1975).

434   Dworkin, Andrea. *Woman Hating*. New York: E. P. Dutton, 1974. 211 p.
A nonscientific study of sexism in specific literary and historical contexts.
Dworkin analyzes fairy tales, two books and a newspaper, Chinese footbinding,
and witchburning to document female oppression. Calls for androgyny, end to
oppressive patriarchal structures. Limited use.

435   Encel, Solomon; Norman MacKenzie; and Margaret Tebbutt. *Women
and Society: An Australian Study*. Melbourne: Cheshire Publishing, 1974.
320 p.
Begins with a cogent review of feminist theory and explores Australian women
in historical perspective, in education, in public life, and at work. The
statistics and specifics apply primarily to Australia, but the conclusions are
universal.

436   Epstein, Cynthia Fuchs, and William J. Goode, eds. *The Other Half:
Roads to Women's Equality*. Englewood Cliffs, N.J.: Prentice-Hall, 1971. 207 p.
A diverse collection of thought-provoking, previously published essays.
Articles are arranged by topic: the position of women today; biology,
psychology, and women's destiny; employment; other societies (Cuba and
USSR); American feminist programs, and proposals for the seventies. Includes
excerpts from such authors as J. Bernard, L. Tiger, K. Millett, A. Rossi, W.
O'Neill, National Organization for Women, and the Redstockings. The
unifying theme is how to accomplish equality; women's current social position
as well as alternative positions are examined.

437   Figes, Era. *Patriarchal Attitudes*. London: Faber and Faber, 1970.
191 p., pb.
An examination of male control over and oppression of women as expressed in
Western ideology. Traces patriarchal ideology in Christian theology,
philosophy, science, and psychology as expressed by Rousseau, a "prime
instigator," Darwin, and Freud, among others (p. 94). "Patriarchal attitudes
can survive intellectual change" and depend both on sexual and psychological
"taboos" (p. 111). A major thesis is that the "rise of capitalism is the root cause
of the modern social and economic discrimination against women" (p. 67).
Figes calls for the abolition of marriage, the "concomitant institution" of
patriarchy, and the commencement of state "responsibility" for children (p.
181). Makes observations and conclusions on basis of excerpts drawn from
anthropological, psychological, philosophical, theological, and historical
writings. Some lack of thorough knowledge of these fields is evident.

438   Freeman, Jo, ed. *Women: A Feminist Perspective*. Palo Alto, Calif.:
Mayfield, 1975. 487 p., pb.
Wide-ranging collection of first-published and reprinted articles on biology,
family relations, socialization, working women (including in professions and

trade unions), female image in various art forms, legal issues, black women, American politics, psychotherapy, history of feminism, current women's liberation movement. Many years in the making; suffers severe lack of focus. Some popular, some scholarly essays; many very good, but available elsewhere. Attempts to combine all aspects into one comprehensive collection.

439 Garskof, Michele Hoffnung, ed. *Roles Women Play: Readings toward Women's Liberation.* Belmont, Calif.: Brooks/Cole, 1971. 210 p., pb.
A collection that aims to show the interrelationship of economic and social factors with women's psychology. Includes articles available elsewhere by C. Bird, N. Weisstein, S. and D. Bem, M. Horner, J. Freeman, A. Rossi, M. Dixon, and M. Benston, among others.

440 Glazer-Malbin, Nona, and Helen Youngelson Waehrer. *Woman in a Man-Made World: A Socioeconomic Handbook.* Chicago: Rand NcNally, 1972. 316 p., pb.
A reader on the contemporary social position of women in the U.S., designed for undergraduate courses. Includes general historical perspectives by W. J. Goode, I. Pinchbeck; a theoretical article by J. Mitchell; contributions on psychobiological aspects of sex differences by Freud, M. J. Sherfey; economic aspects of sex differences by Engels, K. Gough, M. Bernson; socialization by K. Horney and E. Goffman. Other topics include sex-role differentiation, marriage, the job market, and advancement toward sex equality by K. Millett and P. Mainardi. The selections are brief and are prefaced with helpful introductions; some are reprints and others were prepared for this anthology.

441 Huber, Joan, ed. *Changing Women in a Changing Society.* Chicago: University of Chicago Press, 1973. 295 p., pb.
Contributors to this book include J. Bernard, J. Freeman, H. Papanek, M. Komarovsky, C. F. Epstein, V. K. Oppenheimer, S. Feldman, H. Lopata, D. Scully, and P. Bart. The topics range from the origins of the women's liberation movement to how women are presented in gynecology textbooks, and include a variety of approaches to women and work (income differences, relation to marital patterns, sex discrimination in university faculty, successful black professional women, demographics, French professional women) and to women and families/sex roles (swinging as domain of decision-making in marriage, adult sex roles and mental illness, social stratification, marriage and graduate education, black and white widows; includes a review of sex-role research). The chapter by C. Ehrlich on feminist texts is a very useful review of seventeen well-known publications. Overall a wide-ranging, informed collection; also available as *American Journal of Sociology* 78, no. 4 (January 1973).

442 Janeway, Elizabeth. *Between Myth and Morning: Women Awakening.* New York: William Morrow, 1974. 279 p.
Janeway's essays and reviews from popular press and panel discussions on

women. Literate, insightful, personal. Topics include women in management, Freud, families, older women.

443 Janeway, Elizabeth. *Man's World, Woman's Place: A Study of Social Mythology.* New York: William Morrow, 1971. 307 p., pb.
A general discussion of cultural ideology and the subordination of women. Analyzes socially prescribed roles of mother, worker, and wife. Witches through history, the social system, economic roles of women, politics, sexuality, and the feminist movement are examined. Draws on material from sociology, psychoanalytic theory, history, and literature. Presents some provocative ideas.

444 Johnson, Willa D., and Thomas Green. *Perspectives on Afro-American Women.* Washington, D.C.: ECCA, 1975. 187 p., pb.
Nineteen articles on black women in the U.S. from National Conference on Black Women (Louisville, 1974). Includes psychological topics: self-esteem, self-concept, assertiveness; historical topics: slavery; sociological subjects: black family, sex, marriage, "matriarchy," health care, feminist movement. Articles are brief but informative.

445 Kahn, Kathy. *Hillbilly Women.* New York: Doubleday, 1973. 230 p., pb.
Collection of personal stories of women born and raised in the southern Appalachian Mountains, primarily in their own words. Women's activities in unions and community organizing described. Each section is short, interesting, but of limited use.

446 Klein, Viola. *Feminine Character.* London: Routledge and Kegan Paul, 1946. 163 p.
Book devoted to an integrated understanding of Western attitudes and theoretical approaches to the study of women. Material from psychology, sociology, anthropology, philosophy, and history through 1946. Discusses Freud, H. Ellis, A. Adler, H. Thompson, M. Mead, O. Weininger.

447 Komarovsky, Mirra. *Women in the Modern World.* Boston: Little, Brown, 1953. 319 p.
A detailed examination of American women in the 1950s. Analyzes sex roles, socialization, household activities of white middle-class women. Komarovsky argues for women's higher education and development of women's potential. Important for its time, but little present-day relevance.

448 Kristeva, Julia. *About Chinese Women.* Translated by Anita Barrows. London: Marion Boyars, 1977. 203 p.
Based on author's observations and notes from visit to China in 1974; often too personal and simply descriptive. Includes some information on Chinese women's history, and author's view of womanhood in Western society. Originally published in Paris, 1974.

449   Ladner, Joyce A. *Tomorrow's Tomorrow: The Black Woman.* New York: Doubleday, Anchor, 1971. 296 p., pb.
After an introductory chapter on the history of the black family and black women, Ladner presents the results of her research among adolescent black females, and a discussion of black womanhood. Conclusion emphasizes the autonomous social system of the black community and the healthy adjustments made by blacks to conditions not intended to promote their well-being. Includes seven page bibliography.

450   Lakoff, Robin. *Language and Woman's Place.* New York: Harper and Row, 1975. 83 p., pb.
A significant, thought-provoking essay on American language conventions that are sexually differentiated, that illustrate women's inferior position, and that show women's politeness.

451   Lifton, Robert Jay, ed. *The Woman in America.* Boston: Houghton Mifflin, 1965. 293 p., pb.
Essays, many of which first appeared in *Daedalus,* Spring 1964. The topics and contributors include E. H. Erikson on inner and outer space, R. J. Lifton on psychohistorical perspectives, D. Trilling on contemporary literature, D. Riesman on generational differences, A. Rossi on equality between the sexes, E. Peterson on working women, D. C. McClelland on self-image, C. N. Degler on the changing place of women, E. G. Rostow on conflict and accommodation, L. Bailyn on the psychology of professional women, J. Conway on Jane Addams, and J. M. Erikson on Eleanor Roosevelt. Most of the articles are personal essays that attempt to come to general conclusions about all women and womanhood.

452   Martin, Del, and Phyllis Lyon. *Lesbian/Woman.* San Francisco: Glide, 1972. 277 p., pb.
Martin and Lyon present informative discussion of lesbian childhood, image and role, sexuality, life-style, motherhood, and liberation based on insightful personal accounts. Although nonscientific, book provides social analysis. Well written.

453   Miller, Casey, and Kate Swift. *Words and Women.* New York: Doubleday, 1977. 177 p., pb.
An analysis of sexism in the English language. The two authors, free-lance editors, draw on literature, history, anthropology, religion, psychology, and popular media to demonstrate the magnitude of negativity attached to femaleness. They examine names, use of "man," gender of words, polarization of male and female in language, implied meanings of femaleness, "unisex" language, and liberation. Perceive that language demeaning to women is demeaning to men also. Appropriate for undergraduates.

454 Millman, Maurice, and Rosabeth Kanter. *Another Voice: Feminist Perspectives on Social Life and Social Science.* New York: Doubleday, Anchor, 1975. 340 p., pb.
Twelve articles by sociologists on theoretical and research issues in the study of women. Many important contributions include criticisms of scientific models for their emphasis on visible roles of men versus activities of women, for their assumption that men and women "inhabit" similar social worlds, for their emphasis on justification of the status quo instead of development of models for change. Articles on political change, organizations, women and medical sociology, working women, deviance, male gender roles. Articles provide good reviews of relevant literature and extensive bibliographies. Valuable critical analysis of the social scientific study of women. Useful in introductory course.

455 Roszak, Betty, and Theodore Roszak, eds. *Masculine/Feminine: Readings in Sexual Mythology and the Liberation of Women.* New York: Harper and Row, 1969. 307 p., pb.
Twenty-five essays by male sexists, male feminists ("allies"), mid-twentieth-century and 1920s female feminists. Includes excerpts from articles and essays by Freud, L. Tiger, Nietzsche; H. Ellis, G. Myrdal; K. Horney, R. Herschberger, S. de Beauvoir; J. Mitchell, A. Rossi, R. Morgan, G. Rugin, and a collection of manifestos by feminist groups. While many essays are early works, collection as a whole is valuable.

456 Safilios-Rothschild, Constantina, ed. *Toward a Sociology of Women.* Lexington, Mass.: Xerox College Publishing, 1972. 393 p.
Thirty articles on sex roles. Grouped by subject: socialization (findings, factors in differential socialization); stereotypes denigrating to women, exemplified in the media and literature; the "economic subjugation of women to men," demonstrated by Greek dowry and "honor" crimes; the alternatives to "singlehood," and childbearing, academic careers, and political nonparticipation by women; difficulties and solutions for dual-career families; women in nontraditional fields (law, science); the future of the feminist movement in the U.S. and the probability of change in sex roles (p. 101). Collection includes scientific studies, essays, and personal accounts. Highlights important areas of study. Useful at undergraduate level.

457 Sánchez, Rosaura, and Rosa Martinez Cruz, eds. *Essays on La Mujer.* Anthology no. 1. Los Angeles: University of California, Chicano Studies Center Publications, 1977. 194 p., pb.
Twelve articles, mainly by Chicanas, on the political, economic, social, and historical position of Chicanas. Essays on Chicanas and labor force participation, health services, the student movement, and the Chicano family are presented. Themes throughout are class differences between women; failure of the women's liberation movement in U.S. to address issues relevant to the

Chicana; the double oppression of class and sex that Chicanas suffer; cultural nationalism as detracting from the real focus of oppression, that is, capitalism and class society; the necessity of emphasizing economic factors as primary in the oppression of Chicanos. Provides lengthy review and criticism of historical literature on the Chicana, and ten page bibliography. Valuable collection; first of its kind. Appropriate for undergraduates.

458 *Southern Exposure* 4, no. 4 (Winter 1977). "Generations: Women in the South."
An excellent collection of biography, fiction, poetry, photographs, and essays on the experiences of Southern women. Covers the civil rights movement, quilting, rape and lynching, the Southern Summer School for Women Workers, the "Right-to-Life" movement, garden clubs, musicians, and includes six page bibliography.

459 Steiner, Shari. *The Female Factor: A Study of Women in Five Western European Societies.* New York: G. P. Putnam's Sons, 1977. 328 p.
Based on Steiner's residence of more than a decade in Europe; Steiner is obsessed with national character, generalities, and archetypes, as exemplified by chapter titles: "The Englishwoman—The Eternal Teammate"; "The Italian Woman—Matriarchy in Motion"; "The Frenchwoman—'The Other' Nation"; "The German Woman—The New Brunhild"; "The Scandinavian Woman—The Dynamics of Equality." Data on working conditions, marriage, and other social phenomena are included, although book is primarily a personal essay of observation.

460 Stephenson, Mary Lee, ed. *Women in Canada.* Toronto: New Press, 1973. 331 p.
Fifteen articles and extensive bibliography on women by psychologists and sociologists. Topics include women's status, women's rights, socialization, family, marriage, and labor in Canada. Among these articles are analyses of Native American and French Canadian women, women and capitalism, and women in prison. Scholarly, useful text.

461 Thorne, Barrie, and Nancy Henley, eds. *Language and Sex: Difference and Dominance.* Rowley, Mass.: Newbury House, 1975. 311 p.
Twelve articles and a one-hundred page annotated bibliography on sex differences and sexism in language. Emphasis on social context of language and possibilities for change in language use. Contains lengthy overviews of literature on sex and language (B. Thorne, N. Henley) and cross-cultural research on language (A. Bodine); articles on sexism in language (A. Graham, M. Swacker, R. Brend, P. Trudgill), language acquisition (J. Sachs, L. Cherry), differential conversational patterns (D. Zimmerman and C. West). Bibliographical annotations are extremely thorough. Book is basic to study.

462   Weibel, Kathryn. *Mirror Mirror: Images of Women Reflected in Popular Culture.* New York: Doubleday, Anchor, 1977. 256 p., pb.
A general overview of the dominant images of American women in fiction, television, movies, women's magazines, magazine advertising, and in fashion. Primarily describes, instead of analyzes, images through history.

Women and Society

463   Amundsen, Kirsten. *The Silenced Majority: Women and American Democracy.* Englewood Cliffs, N.J.: Prentice-Hall, 1971. 184 p., pb.
A readable investigation into women's power—statistics compiled from all levels of government, trade unions, corporations, and other power foci. Discussion of the ideology of sexism and the effect on a democracy of restricting half the population.

464   Barker, Diana Leonard, and Sheila Allen, eds. *Sexual Divisions and Society: Process and Change.* London: Tavistock, 1976. 286 p.
An excellent collection of scholarly articles about sexual differentiation in society. Writings critically examine traditional approaches to the study of men and women, offering new perspectives, methods of analysis, and conclusions. Some major conclusions: family should be viewed as a "unit producing labour power" (R. Frankenberg); Moroccan women who lack economic autonomy and social mobility create women's networks that directly affect social and political institutions (V. Maher); through education, medicine, social security, marriage, and divorce, society "reinforce[s] sexual differentiation" and inequality (C. Delphy, J. Shaw, S. Macintyre, H. Land, Y. Dezalay) (pp. 4–5). Also articles by M. Brake, D. Davin, P. Abrams, and A. McCulloch, H. Rose, and J. Hanmer. Book's value in its novel perspectives. Important empirical and theoretical contribution.

465   Bernard, Jessie. *Women and the Public Interest.* Chicago: Aldine, 1970. 203 p., pb.
An analysis of the conflict in American society between "public interest" and the "pursuit of happiness," and the role of women. Public interest (government policy) emphasizes "optimum use of each functioning unit," which conflicts with individual expression and development. Official policy does not value potential of women other than for childrearing and ego-support of males. Bernard calls for restructuring the public interest by placing value on intellectual and creative abilities of women.

466   Brownmiller, Susan. *Against Our Will: Men, Women, and Rape.* New York: Simon and Schuster, 1975. 408 p., pb.
A treatise on rape in American society. Examines rape historically, during war,

and of black and Native American women by white men. Examines male homosexual rape in prisons, child abuse, gang rapes, and the ideologies of "heroic" male rapist and passive female victim. Sees male genitalia as weapon used by men to intimidate and oppress women. Views rapists as typical males who do violence to women. Important contribution on a little analyzed topic.

467 Burkhart, Kathryn. *Women in Prison.* New York: Doubleday, 1973. 441 p.
A thorough examination of female prisoners and the penal system. Burkhart presents statistics, descriptions, verbatim interviews, life histories, poetry, photographs, and analyses concerning women prisoners and prison structure. Discusses prisons as component of larger economic-political system in U.S. Valuable study.

468 Chesler, Phyllis, and Emily Jane Goodman. *Women, Money, and Power.* New York: William Morrow, 1976. 259 p.
This book integrates statistics and case studies dealing primarily with middle- and upper-class women. Chapter topics include power, beauty, wealthy women, taxes, marriage and divorce, credit, volunteerism, prostitution, women in the job market, and unions. The lack of ideological focus contributes to the superficiality of some of the discussions (although the authors oppose capitalism and big business, they offer no alternative).

469 DeCrow, Karen. *Sexist Justice.* New York: Random House, Vintage Books, 1975. 363 p., pb.
A scholarly feminist analysis of the legal system—emphasizes the laws, but also covers judges, lawyers, law schools, and legislators. DeCrow examines, and provides specific examples of, sexism in the federal government; the Fourteenth Amendment, wage and employment laws, the Equal Rights Amendment, the education system, and estate, family, criminal, name, and abortion laws are analyzed. Valuable information. Detailed analysis.

470 Diamond, Irene. *Sex Roles in the State House.* New Haven: Yale University Press, 1977.
A study of women and U.S. politics, focusing on women's presence and activities in New England state legislatures. The questionnaire and interviews provided information on combining roles of wife/mother and legislator. Diamond concludes that women's experience is different from men's, and women's equal participation in politics would necessitate a major change in the world generally.

471 Doely, Sarah Bentley, ed. *Women's Liberation and the Church: The New Demand for Freedom in the Life of the Christian Church.* New York: Association Press, 1970. 154 p.

Articles on religious education for women, nuns in women's liberation, history, a Christian perspective on feminism, and women in the ministry.

472   Feldman, Saul D. *Escape from the Doll's House: Women in Graduate and Professional School Education.* New York: McGraw-Hill, 1974. 208 p.
This book on women graduate students is replete with tables illustrating the sexual division of academic disciplines, research activities, career expectations, attitudes toward women, relations with professors and other students, and external constraints on female students. Large amount of useful statistics.

473   Fitzpatrick, Blanche. *Women's Inferior Education: An Economic Analysis.* New York: Praeger, 1976. 189 p.
A thorough investigation of discrimination against women by postsecondary institutions. Includes a discussion of subject matter and schools, a state-by-state analysis of opportunities for women, an examination of economic motives for discrimination, and suggestions for achieving equal educational opportunity.

474   Giallombardo, Rose. *Society of Women: A Study of a Women's Prison.* New York: John Wiley and Sons, 1966. 189 p.
A scientific analysis of a women's prison as a "community" with a "system of roles and functions" (p. vii). Emphasis is on the interaction between and interdependence of roles and functions. Based on one year of intensive research, study describes the prison and presents valuable data on prison staff and prison life, social roles, goals, homosexual alliances, and kinship as means of integration (p. ix).

475   Gornick, Vivian, and Barbara K. Moran, eds. *Women in Sexist Society: Studies in Power and Powerlessness.* New York: Basic Books, 1971. 704 p., pb.
An important collection of feminist articles on beauty, love and marriage, psychology, language, women artists, work, education, and racism. Emphasizes the political nature of woman's condition.

476   Gruberg, Martin. *Women in American Politics: An Assessment and Sourcebook.* Oshkosh, Wis.: Academia Press, 1978. 336 p.
Grunberg summarizes the suffrage movement and resulting women's political activity, and surveys women in government since 1920. Extensive footnotes include lists of names of women in politics. The sourcebook section lists and describes many kinds of American women's organizations. Sixteen page bibliography.

477   Hageman, Alice L., ed. *Sexist Religion and Women in the Church: No More Silence!* New York: Association Press, 1974. 221 p.
A provocative collection of articles on various aspects of women and religion.

Topics include women and the ministry, black women and the church, religious socialization of women, Judeo-Christian influences on female sexuality, nonsexist theology, women in Judaism, women and missions, and sexism in the contemporary church.

478   Howe, Florence. *Women and the Power to Change.* New York: McGraw-Hill, 1975. 127 p., pb.
Four articles by and about women in the university. A. Rich discusses the new "feminist renaissance" in education and the male-centered university that "undermines and exploits" women (pp. 16, 29). A. Hochschild analyzes male-centered academic careers, and discrimination against women in academia. A. Wallach analyzes women and law school, the "archetypal enforcer of social values and class interests hostile to women transmitted by the university" (p. 81). F. Howe discusses female power evidenced in consciousness-raising groups. Howe calls for a concentration of "feminist energy" (in the female-dominated fields of nursing and teaching) as the most constructive means of change. Many valuable concepts put forth.

479   Jaquette, Jane L., ed. *Women in Politics.* New York: John Wiley and Sons, 1974. 367 p.
Important articles on various aspects of women and politics. The first section presents material on women in America: changing patterns of participation (voting and political attitudes); women as political elites; the women's movement; and new alternatives. The second section offers comparative material on women in the Soviet Union, in Chile under Allende, in Costa Rica, in Africa; and articles on some more general topics, for example, "A Marxist Analysis of Women and Capitalism" (T. Kaplan). Most of these very informative articles are previously unpublished.

480   Martin, Del. *Battered Wives.* San Francisco: Glide, 1976. 254 p., pb.
A detailed examination of wife battery as a "natural consequence of women's powerless position vis-à-vis men in patriarchal societies" (p. xii). More specifically, Martin states, "the economic and social structure of our present [patriarchal and capitalist] society depends upon the degradation, subjugation, and exploitation of women" (p. xv). Uses statistics and personal accounts to analyze the incidence of wife battery, motives of the batterer, the victim's reasons (fear, lack of housing, financial support) for returning to or remaining with her husband/batterer, and the inadequacy of existing laws and social services in providing assistance to the women. Last section presents alternatives for women: divorce, reform legislation, and refuges for battered women. A useful combination of social analysis and practical advice.

481   McCourt, Kathleen. *Working Class Women and Grass-Roots Politics.* Bloomington: Indiana University Press, 1977. 256 p.
A sociological analysis of the political activism of white working-class women

in their community, based on interviews with twenty-three active and seventeen nonactive women in Chicago's Southwest Side. Discussion covers the community itself, profiles of the women, their role as community activists, issues and events that got them involved, and the effect of this involvement on their personal and political lives. A readable, informative study of a neglected topic.

482 Milwaukee County Welfare Rights Organization. *Welfare Mothers Speak Out: We Ain't Gonna Shuffle Anymore.* New York: W. W. Norton, 1972. 190 p., pb.
Statistical material from statements by welfare recipients and research. An important book, presents information on the experiences of these seldom-studied women. Includes material on Spanish-speaking people, welfare as a right, welfare myths, and the variety of suggested plans for income redistribution. Appendixes include statistical information. Book is intended to involve people in the struggle for welfare rights.

483 New York Radical Feminists. *Rape: The First Source Book for Women.* Edited by Noreen Connell and Cassandra Wilson. New York: New American Library, 1974. 283 p., pb.
Essays, interviews, articles taken primarily from two conferences on rape held by New York Radical Feminists. Divided into consciousness-raising, "speaking out," feminist analysis of psychosocial aspects of rape, legal issues, and "feminist action," including rape crisis centers, self-defense, political action, health-related issues. Some topics: the "rape tape," psychotherapy and rape (P. Chesler), rape in the media, sexual abuse of children. Rape is regarded as the product of psychological and political oppression. Book addresses many critical issues.

484 Rowbotham, Sheila. *Woman's Consciousness, Man's World.* Baltimore: Penguin, 1973. 136 p., pb.
A clear Marxist discussion of the personal and political situation of women in capitalist society; primarily through descriptions of author's growing awareness. Rowbotham investigates the psychological oppression of women, their work in the home, their industrial labor, the relationship of imperialism to everyday life. An important contribution to socialist-feminist thought.

485 Roy, Maria, ed. *Battered Women: A Psychosociological Study of Domestic Violence.* New York: Van Nostrand Reinhold, 1977. 334 p., pb.
An examination of social, psychological, law enforcement, and legal factors involved in wife battery (refers to men and women involved in an intimate relationship). Nineteen articles variously discuss the husband, the incidence of beating and its effects on women, motivations of women for seeking or not seeking help, response to women by law enforcement and social agencies. Most articles and final section present viable solutions to many aspects contributing to wife beating, including detailed models for refuges and legislation. Thesis is

that several factors contribute to "growth" and "maintenance" of wife beating (p. 25). Clearly written; book provides wealth of information and analysis. Appropriate for undergraduates.

486   Safilios-Rothschild, Constantina. *Women and Social Policy*. Englewood Cliffs, N.J.: Prentice-Hall, 1974, 197 p.
This book synthesizes current information, research, and theories, and describes possibilities for action directed at changing social policy and laws. Topics include theoretical issues in social policy related to women, strategies to liberate women and men from existing constraints (housekeeping, education, economics, psychology), social policy alternatives to "compulsive marriage" and the family, and possible changes in language, therapy, legal system, politics, and religion. Nineteen page bibliography. Often thought-provoking, although some specific strategies are unrealistic.

487   Seifer, Nancy. *Nobody Speaks for Me!: Self-Portraits of American Working Class Women*. New York: Simon and Schuster, 1976. 477 p.
The stories of ten women, told in their words. Women's involvement in political activity, community and union organizing, belie the stereotype of passive women. The women's various backgrounds (different regions of the U.S., urban and rural, black, Chicana, Italian, Jewish) provide an important addition to the understanding of American women.

488   Stacey, Judith; Susan Bereaud; and Jean Daniels; eds. *And Jill Came Tumbling After: Sexism in American Education*. New York: Dell, 1974. 461 p., pb.
Previously published articles covering women's attitudes about education. The sex-role-defining materials used in kindergartens, children's books, sexism in high school and college, teachers, and alternative materials and practices are discussed. Includes a twenty-five page bibliography.

489   Sullerot, Evelyne. *Women, Society and Change*. Translated by Margaret Scotford Archer. London: World University Library, 1971. 252 p.
A general study of women's subordinate position and the move toward their increased participation in "male" spheres of society. Examines "social evolution" of patriarchal system that is dependent upon the isolation of women in the domestic/reproductive sphere; significant differences in men's and women's labor force participation, wages and types of work, overtime; women's access to education and nondiscriminatory legislation; their involvement in politics and the church. Cites demographic factors significant in the development of women's roles as wife, mother, and worker. Relies primarily on statistics. Useful for broad overview of the topic.

490   Tolchin, Susan, and Martin Tolchin. *Clout: Womanpower and Politics*. New York: Coward, McCann and Geoghegan, 1974. 320 p.

A readable study of women and women's issues in regular party politics in the U.S. Illustrated with details from a variety of primarily East Coast political campaigns. Includes specifics on the Equal Rights Amendment victory in Connecticut, the lobbying efforts around credit law reform, the experiences of Bella Abzug, and women in Kevin White's administration (Boston). An interesting overview of changes in the last decade: women's exclusion from politics, their conquest of role obstacles and achievement of political success, and the growth of a strong women's presence in the political arena. Twelve page bibliography.

491   Whitehurst, Carol. *Women in America: The Oppressed Majority.* Santa Monica: Goodyear, 1977. 156 p., pb.
An examination of women's oppression in the U.S. Deals thoroughly with the institutions that oppress women: marriage, education, economy, political and legal systems. Analysis of psychological oppression of women is most valuable. Thesis is that women are "systematically denied access to power and limited in developing [their] potential" (p. 10). A text appropriate for undergraduate study of female role in U.S.

Marriage and Motherhood

492   Bernard, Jessie. *The Future of Marriage.* New York: Bantam Books, 1972. 325 p., pb.
An overview of American marriage, focusing on the concept of two marriages, as perceived by the wife, and by the husband. Includes discussion of past structures, present conditions, and future possibilities, particularly shared roles. Includes an appendix of tables from a variety of sources. Written in a popular style, designed for lay readers.

493   Bernard, Jessie. *The Future of Motherhood.* New York: Dial Press, 1974. 367 p.
An analysis of motherhood as a social institution affected by "technological, political, economic, and ethical" forces (p. vii). Bernard discusses decisions, motivations for childbearing and childrearing; childcare as "motherwork"; women's integration of professional careers and childcare; the effect of technology and government policy on motherhood; the costs of childrearing; prospects for the integration of mother/worker roles. A provocative and informative discussion.

494   Blood, Robert, and Donald Wolfe. *Husbands and Wives.* New York: Free Press, 1960. 269 p., pb.
An analysis of the family based on interviews with 909 black housewives in the Detroit area. Examines domestic decision-making as indicative of a "balance of power" between husbands and wives (p. 23); the success of the family in providing love and affection, emotional and economic support, childrearing,

and companionship for its members; the performance of complementary household tasks by husbands and wives; stresses and satisfactions within the family. While other studies have enlarged upon the scope and analysis of family dynamics of this book, it furnishes important theory and data on the subject.

495 Chapman, Jane Roberts, and Margaret Gates, eds. *Women into Wives: The Legal and Economic Impact of Marriage*. Sage Yearbooks in Women's Policy Studies, vol. 2. Beverly Hills: Sage, 1977. 320 p.
Eleven articles on topics such as socialization, wife beating, federal programs, legal reforms for partnership marriage, health and fertility, black women, childcare, public policy, widows and divorcees, divorce and role change, and mothers in experimental family life-styles. Includes a statistical appendix. An excellent collection, presenting recent provocative research dealing with marital status.

496 Farber, Seymour M., and Roger H. L. Wilson. *The Challenge to Women*. New York: Basic Books, 1966. 176 p.
Symposium on women and population control. Participants include E. Merriam, M. Komarovsky, E. Albert, M. Lerner, D. Lee, P. Sears. Wide-ranging topics include women's expectations; duties of mothers; "natural" motherhood (voluntary childlessness); mother-child and father-son relationships; neighborhoods; psychology of older women. Lacks focus.

497 Gavron, Hannah. *The Captive Wife: Conflicts of Housebound Mothers*. New York: Humanities Press, 1966. 176 p.
A detailed study of a sample (ninety-six) of young married British mothers and their "roles in the modern family" (p. xii). After a general introduction to changes of the past century in women's position legally, politically, and in family structure generally, the different experiences of middle- and working-class women in families are examined. Author's questions center on women's marriages, children, social contacts, division of labor and other aspects of running the house, leisure time, and work.

498 Kohl, Seena B. *Working Together: Women and Family in Southwestern Saskatchewan*. Toronto: Holt, Rinehart and Winston of Canada, 1976. 139 p., pb.
Part of a series of interdisciplinary studies on family, kinship, and marriage, and part of a research project on North American agricultural families. Includes background information on local geography, social esteem, power, role of women in development of social community, social networks and control (kinship, friends, economic exchange). Specific topics include individual life cycles, family roles and relationships, women in the family enterprise. A comparative essay by J. W. Bennett on Hutterite women and their families is provided. Although very specific, book is informative and has potential use in combination with other monographs on families or rural sociology.

499 Komarovsky, Mirra. *Blue Collar Marriage.* New York: Random House, 1967. 356 p., pb.
A sociological analysis of fifty-eight "blue collar" marriages (defined by occupation, income, and education). Covers these topics: conjugal roles, interaction between spouses, conjugal power, extrafamilial kin relations, effects of husband's job on marital relations. Data gathered from interviews (primarily with wives) and systematically analyzed. Many important distinctions (attributed to education) between "blue collar" and "white collar" marriages are discussed. Scholarly source of information on working-class couples.

500 Peck, Ellen, and Judith Senderowitz, eds. *Pronatalism: The Myth of Mom and Apple Pie.* New York: Thomas Y. Crowell, 1974. 332 p., pb.
Articles on parenthood and social pressure (especially by the media) to have children; includes information on voluntary childlessness, some statistical studies on childless marriages, motivation and desire for children, and childlessness and marriage breakdown.

501 Rainwater, Lee; Richard Coleman; and Gerald Handel. *Working Man's Wife: Her Personality, World and Life Style.* New York: Oceana, 1959. 219 p.
A sociopsychological study of five hundred American women married to working-class men. TAT and other projective tests, together with interviews, provide much substantive data on women's daily activities, relationships with husbands, children and friends, expenditure of family income, goals and aspirations, participation in organizations, and attitudes toward government institutions. One goal of study was to delineate contributing factors in "consuming style" of these women in order to "provide some clues regarding how best to reach . . . [them] with advertising and sales messages" (pp. ix, 21). Concludes that these women express desires for "economic and physical security . . . support and affection," and to decorate, to "pretty up [their] world" (p. 215). While study lacks detail on women's perspective, it provides useful information.

502 Scanzoni, John. *Sex Roles, Life Styles, and Childbearing: Changing Patterns in Marriage and the Family.* New York: Free Press. 249 p.
A scholarly study of 3,100 black and white, working and nonworking husbands and wives in ten Midwestern cities. Attempt is made to develop a theoretical model based on sex-role norms and attitudes, and fertility control. Education, religion, age at marriage, marital structure, and female employment are analyzed in their relation to fertility control. Men's and women's perceptions of the female sex role were found to affect family size as much as women's employment. Also, egalitarian, "modern" perceptions of female role were positively correlated with smaller family size. Author states that population control is not merely equivalent to birth control but is affected by sex-role norms. Material is complex, but clear introductions and summaries are provided. Important contribution to theory development.

503 Scanzoni, John. *Sexual Bargaining: Power Politics in the American Marriage.* Englewood Cliffs, N.J.: Prentice-Hall, 1972. 180 p.

An analysis of marriage and husband and wife interaction emphasizing "male-female reward-seeking, reciprocity, and conflict" (p. 3). Thesis is that demand for sex-role equality (originating in reward-seeking) leads inevitably to conflict and change. Hence marital conflict has positive function of initiating change. States that marriage is not becoming obsolete. Examines statistics on marital dissolution, changing marital roles, social exchange as basis for marriage, marital conflict, and alternatives to traditional marriage. Provides important perspective on marriage and family. Appropriate for undergraduates.

504 Scanzoni, Letha, and John Scanzoni. *Men, Women, and Change: A Sociology of Marriage and the Family.* New York: McGraw-Hill, 1976. 504 p.

A textbook designed for undergraduate study of marriage and the family. While it emphasizes traditional theory (social exchange, conflict, process), book presents new theoretical approaches; incorporates contemporary phenomena (gay marriage, single parenthood) into analysis. Attempts to integrate various class, sex, ethnic, cultural, and historical differences in overall analysis. Presents theoretical approaches (symbolic interaction, social exchange, conflict theory, structural functionalism) to socialization, premarital decisions, instrumental (political, economic) and expressive features of marriage and conjugal power, reproduction and childrearing, divorce and aging. A broad, detailed view of marriage and the family that incorporates female perspective. Lengthy bibliography.

505 Skolnick, Arlene, and Jerome H. Skolnick. *Intimacy, Family, and Society.* Boston: Little, Brown, 1974. 598 p.

Forty-one scholarly articles that challenge traditional views of, and present new perspectives on, study of the family. Collection is sequel to Skolnick, *Family in Transition.* Thesis is that the "dilemma" of the family is its conflicting functions of "undermin[ing] family ties and . . . generat[ing] exceptional needs for . . . relationships" (p. 12). Skolnick substitutes a "pluralistic" perspective of family patterns for a view based on the universality of the nuclear family. Articles discuss traditional conceptions and contemporary views of the nuclear family; psychosexual and gender identity development, sexuality and male/female roles in society, marriage; the relation of children to parents, "the prenatal mystique," alternative living patterns (e.g., childlessness, singleness, communal living). Each section has an introduction, and articles are abstracted. Book offers new approach to study of family, incorporating a feminist and "humanist" perspective.

506 Staples, Robert. *The Black Woman in America: Sex, Marriage, and the Family.* Chicago: Nelson-Hall, 1973. 261 p.

A sociohistorical examination of the sexuality, social roles (wife and mother), and liberation of black women. Staples views the oppression of black women, resulting from conflict between men and women, as generated by the white politico-economic power elite. Staples analyzes social, economic, and psychological aspects of sexual development, prostitution, wife/mother role, and relationship of black women to feminist movement in U.S. Presents historical background of these factors. Concludes that black women, while sexually better adjusted, are economically more exploited and oppressed than their white counterparts. Black women need liberating and this is essential to the liberation of all black people. While study is largely a presentation of Staples's observations and analyses, there is a collection of interviews with black women. Book is not comprehensive, but does provide some useful information.

Sex Roles and Socialization

507   Belotti, Elena Gianini. *What Are Little Girls Made Of?: The Roots of Feminine Stereotypes.* 1973. Reprint. New York: Schocken Books, 1976. 158 p.
Includes information on the preference for male children; early childhood; games, toys, and children's literature; educational institutions: nursery, primary, and secondary schools. Examines socialization in Italian cultural context, with Italian examples of similar American patterns. Introduction by M. Mead. British edition is titled *Little Girls: Social Conditioning and Its Effects on the Stereotyped Role of Women during Infancy,* published in 1975 with an introduction by M. Drabble.

508   Brenton, Myron. *The American Male.* Greenwich, Conn.: Fawcett, 1966. 224 p., pb.
An early work on the American male sex role. Draws on history, psychology, anthropology, and literature in examination of masculinity, sexuality, and roles of father and breadwinner. Sees men in conflict with patriarchal system that arbitrarily imbues men with superiority, and with the women's liberation movement. While Brenton acknowledges oppression of both men and women under patriarchy, much of his criticism is directed at the demands made by women striving toward equality.

509   Chafetz, Janet Saltzman. *Masculine/Feminine or Human?: An Overview of the Sociology of Sex Roles.* Itasca, Ill.: F. E. Peacock, 1974. 233 p., pb.
An attempt to highlight the salient issues in the sociology of sex roles. Discusses the innate and learned behavioral and psychological differences between males and females, social stereotypes, socialization, the effects of patriarchy and its concomitant institutions that are "geared to maintaining females in a lower caste position," the validity of sex-role stereotypes for interpersonal relationships, and the prospects for a "society of humans," unrestricted by rigid sex roles (p. 151). Some conclusions are that the relationship between mother and child creates a built-in "power differential"

in the family; that "most cultures reinforce those differences that may be inherent in the genders" (i.e., male tendency toward greater aggression, female proclivity toward nurturance) (p. 28). Incorporation of some outdated material limits book's use.

510   Dahlstrom, Edmund, ed. *The Changing Roles of Men and Women.* Boston: Beacon Press, 1971. 302 p.
Well-written collection on such topics as the family and married women at work, sex roles and the socialization process, parental role division and the child's personality development, positions of men and women in the labor market, employer attitudes to female employees; includes an analysis of the debate on sex roles. Originally published in Swedish in 1962, this collection of essays includes the 1968 U.N. report on the status of women in Sweden.

511   David, Deborah, and Robert Brannon. *The Forty-nine Percent Majority: The Male Sex Role.* Reading, Mass.: Addison-Wesley, 1976, 330 p., pb.
A psychosociological study of the American male sex role. Thirty-seven articles examine the four primary features of the role: 1) "success, status, and the need to be looked up to . . . 2) a manly air of toughness, confidence, and self-reliance . . . 3) aura of aggression, violence, daring," 4) everything that is not ideally feminine (p. 12). The authors analyze the socialization process and make suggestions for future male liberation. Valuable insights. Appropriate for undergraduates.

512   Fasteau, Marc Feigen. *The Male Machine.* New York: McGraw-Hill, 1974. 196 p., pb.
A lawyer's personal account of his experience in the stereotypical male sex role in U.S. Examines characteristics of that role in friendships, family, work, sports, sex, and relationships with women. Describes male friendships as "shallow" and competitive; the family as the place where competition and aggression is encouraged; the sex act as the "ultimate test of masculinity." Male "cult of toughness" is evidenced in government policy. Perceptive and useful book.

513   Filene, Peter Gabriel. *Him/Her/Self: Sex Roles in Modern America.* New York: Harcourt Brace Jovanovich, 1974. 351 p.
A history of changes in sex roles of middle-class American women and men from the late nineteenth century to the present, based on wide reading in the popular media, personal histories (letters, diaries, and private journals), fictional histories, and secondary historical sources. Descriptive and comprehensive.

514   Goldberg, Herb. *The Hazards of Being Male: Surviving the Myth of Masculine Privilege.* New York: Nash, 1976. 200 p.
Based on case histories from therapy sessions, this book discusses many of the

constraints put on men in this society, emphasizing sexual relations, patterns of behavior, orientation to male friendships, and marriage and divorce.

515 Holter, Harriet. *Sex Roles and Social Structure.* Oslo: Universitets for laget, 1970. 299 p.

A comprehensive overview of sex-role differentiation, including theoretical discussion and examination of sex-differentiating norms; nondifferentiating ideologies; sex differences in behavior, with closer examination of political, occupational, and educational behavior; some patterns of sex differentiation; the psychology of maintaining sex differentiation; and the implications of sex differentiation.

516 *Journal of Social Issues* 32, no. 3 (1976). "Sex Roles: Persistance and Change."

Sixteen articles on the maintenance of sex roles and the potential for change. Articles discuss the interrelationship between societal factors (e.g., cultural norms, economy) that perpetuate sex roles, the interaction between psychological (personal attitudes, socialization) and societal constraints, the effect of situational factors (e.g., discrimination) on sex roles, and the need for change. Important theoretical and empirical contributions. Good collection.

517 Komarovsky, Mirra. *Dilemmas of Masculinity: A Study of College Youth.* New York: W. W. Norton, 1976. 274 p.

A study of sixty-two Ivy League college seniors in 1969–1970, their view of masculinity, their role in society, their relationships with women (intellectual and sexual) and with parents. Contains many excerpts from interviews. Uses psychological perspectives to supplement the primarily sociological analysis of the changing role expectations and resulting strains on these men.

518 Konopka, Gisela. *The Adolescent Girl in Conflict.* Englewood Cliffs, N.J.: Prentice-Hall, 1966. 141 p.

A nonscientific sociopsychological study of 181 delinquent adolescent girls. Based on personal interaction with the girls, Konopka posits that lack of economic opportunity, and loneliness, despair, and conflict (stemming from both the physiological changes in adolescents and the movement toward "woman's emancipation") are the primary components of the girls' orientation. Provides many transcribed interviews, some useful material.

519 McGuigan, Dorothy. *New Research on Women and Sex Roles.* Ann Arbor: University of Michigan Center for Continuing Education of Women, 1976. 383 p., pb.

Forty-four articles, primarily by students and graduates of University of Michigan, on women and sex roles. Topics include "changing sex roles," "work, family, and social change," "status, power, and politics," "women and men," women and higher education, literature, and the media. Articles examine women in historical, cross-cultural, and contemporary U.S. contexts. Many good articles, including those by J. Bardwick, S. Harding, and J. Pleck. Good collection.

520   Oakley, Ann. *Sex, Gender, and Society*. London: Temple Smith, 1972. 223 p., pb.
An examination of the biological and cultural bases of sex differentiation. Attempts both critical review of those basic assumptions about sex differentiation, and establishment of the differences between males and females. Discusses biological factors in sex differentiation; sex and personality, intellect, social role and gender; socialization into gender roles. Draws extensively from biology, psychology, and anthropology to substantiate hypotheses. While overall analysis is good, validity of some conclusions is questionable, for example, "to some extent, aggression is biologically determined" and "the different patterns of male and female criminal behavior appear to reflect the male's greater aggressiveness and greater tendency to deviance" (pp. 42, 66). Occasionally cursory understanding of some areas such as psychoanalytic theory is exhibited. Useful, but somewhat dated.

521   Pleck, Joseph, and Jack Sawyer. *Men and Masculinity*. Englewood Cliffs, N.J.: Prentice-Hall, 1974. 184 p.
Brief personal accounts of men in U.S. Includes discussion of male role in family, sports, and work, and interaction with women. Useful data on male role.

522   Reeves, Nancy. *Womankind: Beyond the Stereotypes*. Chicago: Aldine-Atherton, 1971. 425 p.
An overall view of the bases of women's subordinate role in U.S. Examines female role stereotypes in marriage, law, family, work, education, and male/female interaction. Reeves analyzes assumptions on which stereotypes are based: immutability of traditional sex roles and primary determination of behavior by anatomy. Presents "parallel readings" on topics of women and work, marriage, politics, and psychology. Also feminist and antifeminist writings. Book's scope renders the study useful for overview of sex roles, but it is limited as a source of data and scientific analysis.

523   Ribal, Joseph. *Learning Sex Roles: American and Scandinavian Contrasts*. San Francisco: Canfield Press, 1973. 267 p.
Thirty-six examples of Swedish, Danish, and American university students' recollections of their sexual socialization. Short narratives that focus on experiences in childhood, adolescence, and young adulthood are preceded by author's summary of concomitant psychological developmental stages. Descriptions are followed by discussion. Narratives are frank and provide valuable data.

524 Seward, Georgene, and Robert Williamson. *Sex Roles in Changing Society*. New York: Random House, 1970. 406 p.
An attempt to evaluate sex roles in African "primitive societies" and in the U.S., Latin America, Germany, the USSR, Greece, India, Japan, and China. Articles by anthropologists, sociologists, and psychologists. Much of the material and consequent analyses are outdated. Some sexist, racist, and ethnocentric overtones. Limited use.

525 Snodgrass, Jon, ed. *A Book of Readings for Men against Sexism*. Albion, Calif.: Times Change Press, 1977. 238 p., pb.
Fifteen articles and a brief selected bibliography on men and their struggle against patriarchal oppression of women and men. Largely descriptive, articles and essays are variously personal accounts, political-social analyses, and assessments (most by men, some by women) of male antisexist movement, male dominance, male sexuality, and oppression (by sex, class, and race) of women and men. Includes review of J. Pleck's *Men and Masculinity* (C. Ehrlich); criticism of film *Men's Lives* (J. Snodgrass); statements by men's liberation groups and gay male groups, and an analysis of "liberated men" (K. Grimstad and S. Rennie). Editor points to absence of analysis of sources of oppression and of analysis of relation between sex, race, and class oppression. Book is not a theoretical contribution, but does supply most thoughtful descriptive essays on sexism to date.

526 Stoll, Clarice Stasz. *Female and Male: Socialization, Social Roles, and Social Structure*. Dubuque: William C. Brown, 1974. 209 p., pb.
An analysis of sociosexual differentiation in U.S. Emphasizes biological differences delineated by scientific research. Examines socialization of sexes, sexism in U.S. and in the social sciences. Sections on male/female roles, "surviving," and "coping and [the] consequences." Deals critically and analytically with scientific data.

527 Stoll, Clarice Stasz, ed. *Sexism: Scientific Debates*. Reading, Mass.: Addison-Wesley, 1973. 121 p.
Eight articles that discuss the origins and manifestations of sexism in the U.S. Authors analyze physiological sex differences (J. Money), childhood sex differences (J. Bardwick), game strategies of men and women (C. Stoll), "male bonding" (L. Tiger), women's careers and social norms (J. Bernard). Most concepts presented have been modified by recent research, but work constitutes valuable collection.

528 West, Uta. *Women in a Changing World*. New York: McGraw-Hill, 1975. 170 p.
Fourteen essays and short stories about female and male experience, primarily in U.S. Contains works by D. Lessing, E. Janeway, A. Nin. Discussion of

psychological reactions to and difficulties with "liberation"; emotional component of change and self-awareness analyzed. Good collection.

Contemporary Feminist Thought

Introduction

This section is designed to present important material that does not readily fall into one of the academic areas, particularly theoretical contributions on the present women's movement. The General subsection includes studies on special aspects of the feminist movement, such as medical questions, lesbianism, theoretical discussions, and the new classics. The Feminist Movement has writings from and about the movement itself, including some sociological and political studies based on research into the organization and dynamics of feminism. Contributions on these topics increase regularly; we have listed here some of the seminal materials that are vital to an understanding of the new feminism.

General

529   Abbott, Sidney, and Barbara Love. *Sappho Was a Right-On Woman: A Liberated View of Lesbianism.* New York: Stein and Day, 1972. 251 p., pb.
A pioneer essay on lesbianism. Focus of discussion is the "struggle" between "shame and pride." Includes description of social oppression. Presents new ways of perceiving lesbianism, emphasizing self worth and cultural change, and includes discussion of relationship between gay liberation, National Organization for Women, and the American feminist movement. Although the authors tend to generalize, book is significant for its time and presents important material.

530   Allen, Pamela. *Freespace: A Presentation on the Small Group in Women's Liberation.* Albion, Calif: Times Change Press, 1970. 63 p., pb.
A discussion of small group dynamics based on Allen's involvement in an early feminist group, Sudsofloppen, in San Francisco. Designed as a handbook and guide for others interested in organizing or participating in small political discussion groups.

531   Altbach, Edith Hoshino, ed. *From Feminism to Liberation.* Cambridge, Mass.: Schenkman, 1971. 275 p.
A collection of articles from a socialist perspective, including a useful introduction to recent women's history. Includes poems, essays, and investigative articles, such as M. J. Buhle on the Socialist party, 1901–1914, and J. Mitchell's "The Longest Revolution." Many selections were previously published in the February 1970 issue of *Radical America.*

532   Cade, Toni, ed. *The Black Woman: An Anthology.* New York: New American Library, Mentor Books, 1974. 256 p., pb.
An excellent collection of essays and fiction by and about black women. Discusses their experiences with black men, as children, and as activists; examines racism and sexism; shows concern about education and birth control. The many contributors include N. Giovanni, A. Walker, F. Beal, and A. Lincoln.

533   Davis, Elizabeth Gould. *The First Sex.* Baltimore: Penguin, 1971. 382 p., pb.
A discussion of women's history that presents matriarchy as a past reality and as "the only hope for the survival of the human race" (p. 18). Misuses anthropological and historical sources, and relies to some extent on such nineteenth-century authorities as Bachofen. Useless and polemical.

534   Diner, Helen. *Mothers and Amazons: The First Feminine History of Culture.* New York: Julian Press, 1965. 289 p.
A treatise on the existence of matriarchy in Greece, India, Asia, Tibet, Malaysia, Central and South America, Egypt, and North America. Cites evidence from myths, symbols, and cosmology in which women are portrayed as goddesses and queens. Draws extensively on Bachofen and Briffault. Scientific analysis is absent.

535   Edward, Lee R.; Mary Heath; and Lisa Baskin. *Women: An Issue.* Boston: Little, Brown, 1972. 299 p.
An eclectic collection of history, poetry, personal essays, analytic essays, paintings (including a series of women artists' self-portraits), literary criticism, and fiction. Originally published as *Massachusetts Review* 13, nos. 1, 2.

536   Eisenstein, Zillah R., ed. *Capitalist Patriarchy and the Case for Socialist Feminism.* New York: Monthly Review Press, 1979 [1978]. 304 p.
A significant contribution to and synthesis of feminist and Marxist theories. Seventeen articles critically examine and substantially refine concepts of patriarchy, capitalism, and feminism, and demonstrate the intricate relationship of all three. Based generally on thesis that there exists a "mutually reinforcing dialectical relationship between capitalist class structure and hierarchical sexual structuring," articles explore components of socialist-feminist theory and capitalist patriarchy (Z. Eisenstein), feminist theory (N. Harstock), "mothering," patriarchy, and capitalism (N. Chodorow), reproductive freedom (L. Gordon), suffrage movement (E. DuBois), femininity and capitalism in antebellum U.S. (M. Ryan), domestic labor (J. Gardiner), monopoly capitalism and consumption (B. Weinbaum, A. Bridges), sexual segregation of jobs (H. Hartmann), clerical labor force (M. Davies), Cuban women (C. Bengelsdorf, A. Hageman), Cuban family code (M. Randall), Chinese family revolution (J. Stacey); also includes statements by Berkeley-

Oakland Women's Union and Combahee River Collective and assessment of Marxist-feminist groups (R. Petchesky) (p. 5). Book is critical to study of women in all fields and constitutes major work in socialist-feminist theory.

537 Firestone, Shulamith. *The Dialectic of Sex: The Case for Feminist Revolution.* New York: William Morrow, 1970. 424 p., pb.
An important contribution to radical feminist theory; includes provocative chapters on American feminism, Freudianism, childhood, racism, love, romance, and male culture. Firestone's discussion leads to the conclusion that structural social change is dependent on changing biological functions, specifically the development of "test-tube babies," her most controversial demand. This book remains a seminal work, providing a starting point for discussion of a variety of topics.

538 Frankfort, Ellen. *Vaginal Politics.* New York: Quadrangle/New York Times, 1972. 224 p., pb.
A scathing description of current medical practice concerning women; advocates women's control of their own bodies. Frankfort is objective, however, and does not advocate actions for political reasons alone. Includes discussion of structural change in the health care system. There are fine, informative chapters on sperm banks, abortion, drugs (media and drug industry), cancer, VD, health care in China, psychiatrists, and sex manuals (especially Dr. Reuben's). Still very relevant, though some specifics have changed in the past five years.

539 Friedan, Betty. *The Feminine Mystique.* New York: Dell, 1963. 364 p., pb.
A pioneer study of women's oppression in the U.S. Friedan analyzes the false aura of happiness and fulfillment, perpetuated by social values and the media, that surrounds the white middle-class housewife. Results of the negation of women's intellect and creativity inherent in housework, she argues, include neurosis, suicide, passive daughters, homosexual sons, divorce, and loss of identity. Although limited in scope, this book is of great historical importance.

540 Galana, Laurel, and Gina Covina. *The New Lesbians: Interviews with Women across the U.S. and Canada.* Berkeley: Moon Books, 1977. 223 p., pb.
Twenty interviews with lesbians conducted by Galana and Covina, themselves lesbians. Although the verbatim interviews are not analyzed in detail, they provide much valuable information. Authors observe that, with the exception of two relationships (from estimated one hundred), "role-playing" among the women was absent. Book's utility lies in its abundance of detail from participants' experiences.

541 Gould, Carol C., and Marx W. Wartofsky, eds. *Women and Philosophy: Toward a Theory of Liberation.* New York: Capricorn Books, 1976. 364 p.

A thorough, excellent collection based on a special issue of *Philosophical Forum* 5, no. 1–2. The essays are arranged in four sections: methodological issues, historical critique, analysis and critique of the present, and future possibilities. The themes these essays address include the question of "women's nature," exploitation and oppression of women, principles that guide practical action aimed at the liberation of women, and the relationship of women's liberation with other social groups. Highly recommended for courses in philosophy, and for better understanding of applications of philosophy to feminism.

542   Greer, Germaine. *The Female Eunuch.* New York: Bantam Books, 1970. 353 p., pb.
A witty essay on the debasement of the American female which posits that women are "castrated" by virtue of their sexual exploitation and their socialization into a denial of their mental and creative potential. A woman's self-concept is based on vicarious experience through husband's and children's achievements. Greer calls for a revolution of social values.

543   Guettel, Charnie. *Marxism and Feminism.* Toronto: Canadian Women's Educational Press, 1974. 62 p., pb.
An essay in two parts: the first is a useful Marxist critique of feminist writings, the second attempts to incorporate feminist ideology into a Marxist framework. This is not a discussion of new socialist-feminist theory.

544   Hays, H. R. *The Dangerous Sex.* New York: Pocket Books, 1964. 297 p., pb.
A nonscientific examination of male hostility toward and fear of women based on male envy of female reproductive capacities. Hays offers evidence from myths, anthropological data, and psychoanalytic theory. Credibility is lacking.

545   Johnston, Jill. *Lesbian Nation: The Feminist Solution.* New York: Simon and Schuster, 1973. 283 p., pb.
A mixture of autobiography and sociosexual-political analyses of lesbianism. Johnson describes her experiences growing up in the 1950s, her confrontation with the women's liberation movement of the 1960s, development of her sexual identity and political consciousness. She analyzes lesbian feminism, the gay movement and women's oppression in male-dominated society. Characterizes lesbians as those women who have integrated the "personal and the political" in their struggle against male oppression (p. 276). Views "going straight" as "legitimizing your oppression" (p. 276). Represents early important work on lesbian feminism.

546   Komisar, Lucy. *The New Feminism.* New York: Franklin Watts, 1971. 181 p.
Designed as a text for high school women or younger this book discusses

sexism, the socialization process, work segregation, abortion, legal issues, history, the rebirth of the women's movement, and the international struggle in an informative though elementary way.

547 Luria, Gina, and Virginia Tiger. *Everywoman.* New York: Random House, 1976. 162 p.
A collection of literary and historical notations and photographs on women and childbirth, violence, "seduction," education, physical appearance, singleness and marriage, sexuality, work, and death in a general historical context. Book emphasizes stereotypes of women in these facets of life, without presenting a critical analysis of stereotypes or their bases. A main theme throughout is women's potential for violence against men and other women. Book has little value in classroom.

548 Martin, Wendy, ed. *The American Sisterhood: Writings of the Feminist Movement from Colonial Times to the Present.* New York: Harper and Row, 1972. 374 p., pb.
This collection is divided into sections: 1) political, legal, and economic issues, and 2) social, sexual, and psychological questions, with the internal arrangement chronological. Includes selections from A. Hutchinson's trial and essays by E. C. Stanton, C. Eastman, G. Steinem, F. Wright, M. Sanger, M. Horner, R. Morgan. A potentially useful juxtaposition of a variety of writings.

549 Millett, Kate. *Sexual Politics.* New York: Avon Books, 1969. 393 p., pb.
An analysis of women's subordination to male political control in patriarchy, especially in the family. The wife/prostitute is forced into economic and psychological dependency through the surrender of her autonomy and identity to the dominating male. Millett analyzes the exploitative male attitudes toward women in the works of H. Miller, D. H. Lawrence, N. Mailer, and Freud. Also examines the writings of J. S. Mill and J. Genet as challenges to the concept of inherent inferiority of women. An early, thought-provoking feminist document.

550 Mitchell, Juliet. *Woman's Estate.* New York: Random House, Vintage Books, 1971. 182 p., pb.
This important contribution to socialist-feminist theory describes the recent historical and political background of women's liberation, connections of the women's movement with minority liberation movements, and the radical influences of the 1960s. Mitchell's theoretical discussion is a serious and demanding evaluation of Marxism and Freudian psychoanalysis and what they have to offer to a theory of women's liberation. The discussion focuses on production, reproduction, sexuality, and socialization. A ground-breaking synthesis.

551   Montagu, Ashley. *The Natural Superiority of Women.* 1953. Reprint. New York: Collier, 1974. 250 p., pb.
An examination of differences between men and women which concludes that women are biologically superior based on their resistance to disease, emotional durability, faster response to stimuli, high performance on IQ tests, and lower incidence of alcoholism and suicide. Also discusses male womb envy, oppression of women in American society, and sexual responses of men and women. Scientific data is used to support these hypotheses, but book lacks analysis.

552   Morgan, Elaine. *The Descent of Woman.* New York: Stein and Day, 1972. 258 p.
A somewhat fictionalized undocumented account of the evolution of humans from apes. Relies on primate behavior to explain human behavior, and presents hazy generalities.

553   Phelps, Stanlee, and Nancy Austin. *The Assertive Woman.* Fredericksburg, Va.: Impact/Bookcrafters, 1975. 177 p., pb.
A guide to changing behavior patterns, to become assertive (not aggressive) in daily encounters. Designed as a practical tool for use in workshops; includes examples of reactions to various experiences. Very helpful suggestions and comments.

554   *Radical Teacher: A Newsjournal of Socialist Theory and Practice* 6 (December 1977). "Women's Studies in the 70s: Moving Forward."
Fifteen articles about teaching women's studies, recent research, and the status of women's studies curricula/programs. Provides both scholarly analyses and practical advice for instructors. Articles include Afro-American literature (G. Hull), studying lesbian culture (T. McNaron), an inside view of *Signs* (C. Stimpson, editor), "Feminism in the Bible Belt" (J. Jones), Southern women's folklore (R. Green), female prisoners' poetry (A. McGovern, editor), teaching in a New York community college (N. Maghn) and at an alternative school (A. Steinberg), and experiences of a white socialist-feminist teaching courses on Third World women (M. Strobel). A useful tool for instructors and researchers.

555   Reed, Evelyn. *Problems of Women's Liberation.* New York: Pathfinder Press, 1970. 96 p., pb.
An analysis of women's oppression as a product of capitalism and as exemplified by monogamy, patriarchy, and private property. Reed points to matriarchy and "primitive communism" as the precursors of monogamy and eventual takeover by the patriarchal order. Calls for an end to class society and capitalism. Thesis supported with some unsubstantiated data regarding matriarchy in an attempt to justify the present struggle for women's liberation.

556 *Social Science Journal* 14, no. 2 (April 1977). "Women's Studies: Awakening Academe."
Eleven articles by professors in various disciplines on the academic study of women. Emphasizes both general appraisal of women's studies and new research on women. Includes sociological analysis of birth (M. Stewart, P. Erickson), cross-cultural examination of menopause (J. Griffen), and detailed evaluations of problems and future of women's studies. Useful for instructors.

557 Watson, Barbara Bellow, ed. *Women's Studies: The Social Realities.* New York: Harpers College Press, 1976. 255 p., pb.
A collection of basic readings on the female perspective in sociology, anthropology, psychology, the feminist movement in the U.S., and feminist thought in the twentieth century. Geared toward the undergraduate, material highlights important areas of study in each field, incorporating excerpts from significant works. Bibliographies and topics for further study are also offered. Clearly written. Extremely useful for introductory, cross-disciplinary women's studies courses.

558 Wysor, Bettie. *The Lesbian Myth.* New York: Random House, 1974. 409 p.
A nonscientific study of lesbianism in Christianity, the sciences, literature, and in the lives of professional women. Wysor analyzes both positive and negative contributions made historically by the church; and in biology, psychiatry, anthropology, and literature. In the second part she presents transcriptions of discussions by lesbians about their life-styles, sexuality, motherhood, and liberation. Provides some good information and analysis.

559 Young, Tracy. *Women Who Love Women.* New York: Pocket Books, 1977. 222 p., pb.
Sixteen biographical sketches of lesbians. Selections from interviews, commentary, and some overall analysis describe lesbian sexuality and life-styles. Many aspects of lesbian experience are covered. Readable. Useful at undergraduate level.

The Feminist Movement

560 *Asian Women.* Berkeley: University of California, 1971. 144 p., pb.
Forty articles, personal essays, and poems collected by Asian women at Berkeley. Divided into "Herstory," Third World women, "politics of womanhood," and "reflections." Some contributions: six years spent in a tiger cage, working in a cannery, Chinese and Japanese immigrant women, women in Japanese literature, women's participation in revolutionary struggles. Includes a lengthy, briefly annotated bibliography. Value of collection is not diminished by its age.

561   Babcox, Deborah, and Madeline Belkin, eds. *Liberation Now: Writings from the Women's Liberation Movement.* New York: Dell, 1971. 382 p., pb.
A useful collection of previously printed articles on a variety of topics, including job discrimination; family life; caste, class, and race; women's culture; woman's control of her body; and international women. Several "classics" are included: N. Weisstein's "Psychology Constructs the Female," A. Koedt's "Myth of the Vaginal Orgasm," P. Mainardi's "Politics of Housework," and others.

562   Bluh, Bonnie Charles. *Woman to Woman: European Feminists.* New York: Starogubski Press, 1974. 317 p., pb.
Bluh's impressionistic account of her year of experiences meeting European feminists. Bluh visited Ireland, England, Holland, France, Italy, and Spain. Her account is primarily based on conversations with individual women; she includes a quantity of information on her own (American) life and her growing feminist consciousness, as well as personal details of her travels. Interspersed is statistical and factual information.

563   Bunch, Charlotte, and Nancy Myron. *Class and Feminism: A Collection of Essays from The Furies.* Baltimore: Diana Press, 1974. 90 p.
Seven essays, written in 1972 by The Furies, a lesbian/feminist collective, that describe personal experience of being female, working class, and middle class in U.S. Article by C. Bunch and C. Reid is detailed examination of aspects of middle-class women's oppression of working-class women. Some of these factors: paternalism, "privileged passivity," "glorif[ication]" of working women's lives, "downward mobility" (pp. 73, 80). Some useful material.

564   Carden, Moren Lockwood. *The New Feminist Movement.* New York: Russell Sage Foundation, 1974. 234 p.
A sociological study of the women's liberation movement in America, based on extensive interviewing and wide reading in the feminist press. Carden accurately outlines the ideas and issues involved, the process of commitment, radicalism, the historical development of the new feminism, activities undertaken by feminists, the variety of organizational forms of women's groups, and the national presence and internal organization of the National Organization for Women. Appendixes include an essay on the author's methodology, lists of organizations, and a select sixteen page bibliography. One limitation is that the only discussion of socialist feminism is in relation to the Socialist Workers party, though the book is otherwise very informative.

565   Cooke, Joanne; Charlotte Bunch-Weeks; and Robin Morgan, eds. *The New Woman: A Motive Anthology on Women's Liberation.* New York: Bobbs-Merrill, 1970. 196 p.
A collection of articles originally published in *Motive*, March–April 1969, plus

some additional articles, and letters in response to that issue. Includes C. Ozich on literary criticism, M. Dixon on liberation, F. Beal on black women, S. Sutheim on women's magazines, D. Martin and P. Lyon on lesbianism, M. S. Webb on American women's roles, A. Howley with a man's view, N. Weisstein with Kinder, Kuche, Kirche, L. Seese on women in leftist politics, C. Bunch-Weeks on issues and actions of women's liberation, a W.I.T.C.H. document, and many poems. An early, excellent collection.

566   Cudlipp, Edythe. *Understanding Women's Liberation*. New York: Paperback Library, 1971. 220 p., pb.
A superficial report on the modern women's movement. Frequently uses the term *girl* to describe women (see p. 20, "women's lib gal"). Aimed at women who are probably not sympathetic, and this discussion will not convince anyone or increase anyone's understanding.

567   Freeman, Jo. *The Politics of Women's Liberation: A Case Study of an Emerging Social Movement and Its Relation to the Policy Process*. New York: David McKay, 1975. 268 p., pb.
A thorough review of the origins of the feminist movement and its effect on public policy formulation. Includes discussion of the National Organization for Women, small groups, the proliferation of media stories and women's organizations, and congressional and governmental agencies' policy decisions. Information ends circa 1974; thus some important recent developments are omitted (antiabortion decision, socialist feminism). Useful because it places material in theoretical framework of the sociological study of social movements and the political science of public policy.

568   Hole, Judith, and Ellen Levine. *Rebirth of Feminism*. New York: Quadrangle/New York Times, 1971. 488 p.
After a brief historical introduction, the authors discuss the origins and growth of the new women's movement; feminist interpretations of ideas about biological differences, social image, and socialization; and "areas of action": mass media, abortion, childcare, education, professions, and the church. Includes a chronology, beginning with 1961; some historical documents; and a twenty page annotated bibliography of books and articles compiled by L. Cisler. A thorough discussion of the development of organization and ideology; includes extensive quotes from ephemeral documents.

569   Koedt, Anne; Ellen Levine; and Anita Rapone, eds. *Radical Feminism*. New York: Quadrangle/New York Times, 1973. 424 p., pb.
A collection of reprints from *Notes from the First, Second,* and *Third Year,* and other sources. Includes sections on history, women's experience, theory analysis, building a movement, and the arts. Many frequently reprinted and well-known articles appear here. It is an important collection nonetheless,

presenting both theory and practice from the radical feminist political view, and providing selections on lesbian politics.

570   Morgan, Robin, ed. *Sisterhood Is Powerful.* New York: Random House, 1970. 594 p., pb.
Articles by journalists, poets, and women active in feminist movement. Focuses on documentation of social and psychological sexism, and social change. Includes essays on professional women, consciousness-raising, prostitution, housework, black and Chicana women, poetry, and high school women. Morgan's introductory thesis is that sexism transcends "class, race, age, and geography." Also, "capitalism, imperialism, and racism are symptoms of male supremacy—sexism" (p. xxxiv). Much valuable information in articles, and a useful bibliography.

571   Reid, Inez Smith. *"Together" Black Women.* New York: Third World Press, 1972. 381 p., pb.
A study initiated by the Black Women's Community Development Foundation that focuses on the views of selected black "miliant" women in the U.S. Transcribed interviews on feminist movement, Pan-Africanism, political ideologies (Marx, Mao, black capitalism), black militancy, and ideas on the future of black liberation movement in the U.S. Author provides background on interview topics and analyzes interview discussions. Insightful and useful.

572   Salper, Roberta, ed. *Female Liberation: History and Current Politics.* New York: Alfred A. Knopf, 1972. 246 p., pb.
An informative and useful collection of documents on the feminist movements of the nineteenth century and of the present; includes a personal essay on the author's own changing consciousness. Early contributors include M. Wollstonecraft, H. T. Mill, F. Douglass, C. P. Gilman, E. Goldman, and others; recent contributors include M. Dixon, R. Dunbar, F. Beal, M. Tax, the Fourth World Manifesto, and others.

573   Tanner, Leslie B., ed. *Voices from Women's Liberation.* New York: New American Library, Signet, 1970. 445 p., pb.
An excellent anthology that includes documents and essays. The historical section includes works by A. Adams, E. C. Stanton, S. B. Anthony, Sojourner Truth, many others. The section on the present includes the Redstocking's Manifesto, a variety of other radical feminist documents and articles, and practical guides to public speaking and to organizing. There are also sections on myths about women (A. Koedt, E. Reed, others), families and day care (L. Gordon, others), high school women, consciousness-raising, radical feminism, theoretical analyses (B. Warrior, N. Weisstein, others), personal accounts, and analyses of the movement (Bread and Roses, S. Firestone, others).

574 Thompson, Mary Lou, *Voices of the New Feminism*. Boston: Beacon Press, 1970. 246 p., pb.
A collection from the early days of the present movement; includes articles on history, sociology, current status of women, and alternatives, and L. Cisler's bibliography. Contributors include B. Friedan, A. Rossi, R. Dunbar, M. Griffiths, M. Daly, C. Bird, S. Chisholm, and P. Murray.

575 Vidal, Mirta. *Chicanas Speak Out: Women—New Voice of La Raza*. New York: Pathfinder Press, 1971. 15 p., pb.
Presentation of First Chicana National Conference, May 1971. Includes essay by Vidal and resolutions passed at conference. Essay analyzes Chicanas' oppression as part of capitalist system in U.S. Provocative and informative.

576 Wandor, Michelene, comp. *The Body Politic: Writings from the Women's Liberation Movement in Britain, 1969–1972*. London: Stage 1, 1972. 261 p.
Variety of articles and ephemeral literature from the movement. Includes recent history and analysis of various aspects of women's experience—family, work, crime, political action. Interesting, although much of it is specific to Britain.

577 Ware, Cellestine. *Woman Power: The Movement for Women's Liberation*. New York: Tower, 1970. 176 p., pb.
A detailed history of the present women's movement, particularly the radical groups (as opposed to National Organization for Women). Includes a chapter on the relationship of black women to the feminist movement, and a theoretical "analysis of contemporary feminism" and of some issues (abortion, mass media, language). Ends with a discussion of some problems of nineteenth-century feminism. Generally a useful, forthright, politically informed book.

578 Williams, Maxine, and Pamela Newman. *Black Women's Liberation*. New York: Pathfinder Press, 1970. 15 p., pb.
Two essays on the position of black women in U.S. Discusses historical features of their experience and need for black women's alliance in their working-class struggle. Brief but informative.

Bibliographies

579 Al-Qazzaz, Ayad. *Women in the Arab World: An Annotated Bibliography*. Association of Arab-American University Graduates, Bibliography series, no. 2. Sacramento: California State University, 1975.
Lengthy annotations of ninety-five sources on Arab women; primarily women in Islam. Includes books, articles, and chapters from books.

580   Astin, Helen S.; Allison Parelman; and Anne Fisher. *Sex Roles: A Research Bibliography*. Rockville, Md.: National Institute of Mental Health, 1975. 362 p., pb.
Annotated bibliography of books, articles, and papers, primarily from 1960 to 1972, covering descriptive studies of observed sex differences, studies of the origins of sex differences, the development of sex roles, and the expression of sex roles, overviews and historical (including cross-cultural) accounts and general reviews, and theoretical position papers. Very useful guide to available material. Contains subject and author index.

581   Astin, Helen S.; Nancy Suniewick; and Susan Dweck. *Women: A Bibliography on Their Education and Careers*. Washington, D.C.: Human Service Press, 1971. 243 p., pb.
Focuses on women's educational and occupational status in the U.S. Each selection has a lengthy abstract, and the editors have included interpretive essays. The three hundred and fifty citations are grouped as follows: determinants of career choice, marital and familial status of working women, women in the world of work, developmental studies, history and economics of women at work, commentaries and policy papers, continuing education, and miscellaneous. Includes books, articles, conference papers, theses, and author and subject indexes.

582   Bickner, Mei Liang. *Women at Work: An Annotated Bibliography*. Los Angeles: University of California, Manpower Research Center, 1974. Unpaged, pb.
Books and articles organized by topic: general, history, education and training, working women (statistics, characteristics, earning unions, attitudes), occupations (professions, academia, management, public employment, clerical, sales and service, semi- and unskilled trades), special groups (youth, mothers, older women, minorities), public policy (federal, Equal Employment Opportunity Commission, court decisions, National Labor Relations Board, law review articles); includes a bibliographies section. Indexed by author, title, cross-reference of categories, and key word. Readability suffers from use of computer, which divides entries at confusing points. Evaluates usefulness. Particularly good on public policy.

583   Bullough, Vern L.; W. Dorr Legg; W. Elcano Barrett; and James Kepner. *An Annotated Bibliography of Homosexuality*. Vol. 2. New York: Garland, 1976. 468 p.
A continuation of volume one. Covers biography and autobiography, literature and art, fiction, poetry, the "homophile movement," periodicals, transvestism, and transsexualism. This collection of listings for 7,218 books and articles contains both an author index and a twenty-five page history of the homophile movement (1948–1960) by S. Licata. Valuable resource.

584   Buvinic, Mayra. *Women and World Development: An Annotated Bibliography*. Washington, D.C.: Overseas Development Council, 1976. 160 p.
Compiled under the auspices of the American Association for the Advancement of Science, the 381 works listed emphasize "the effects of socio-economic development and cultural change on women and women's reactions to these changes" (p. vii). Organized by subjects, further by geographic area; includes rural women, education, women's work, health, associations, and law and politics. Includes list of journals, other bibliographies, and author index. Emphasizes monographs and articles, particularly those from government agencies. Includes twenty page critical essay on the available research.

585   Cabello-Argandoña, Roberto; Juan Gómez-Quiñones; and Patricia Herrera Durán. *The Chicana: A Comprehensive Bibliographic Study*. Los Angeles: University of California, Aztlan Publications, 1976. 200 p.
A collection of 491 articles, books, periodicals on the Chicana. Includes many sources on general topics of women in the U.S. Describes nine films on the Chicana. References divided into serials, general readings, the Chicana and women's liberation, civil rights, culture and cultural processes, folk culture, economics, family, marriage and sex roles, history, education, politics, religion, labor, health, and nutrition. Most references are unannotated articles.

586   Common Women Collective. *Women in U.S. History: An Annotated Bibliography*. Cambridge, Mass.: Common Women Collective, 1976. 114 p., pb.
Arranged by topic and chronologically, beginning with anthologies, general surveys, historiography, resources on Native American women, colonial women, American Revolution, black women, abolitionism and feminism, suffrage, temperance, pioneers, Southern white women, sexuality, social reform, institutions, socialism, the depression, family, Chicanas, lesbians, contemporary women, women at work (arranged by occupation), autobiographies, and references. The critical annotations are extremely useful, written from feminist and radical political perspectives. They note usefulness of book or article for introductory-level and high school courses. Cross-referenced from section to section.

587   Council of Planning Librarians. *Special Issues of Serials about Women, 1965–1975*. Exchange Bibliographies, no. 995. Monticello, Ill.: Council of Planning Librarians, March 1976. 41 p., pb.
A comprehensive annotated listing, excluding only general women's magazines and issues on individual women. Arranged alphabetically by title. Includes many little-known and alternative journals and some international publications.

588   Council of Planning Librarians. *Women and Geography: An Annotated Bibliography and Guide to Sources of Information.* Exchange Bibliographies, no. 1159. Monticello, Ill.: Council of Planning Librarians, 1976. 17 p., pb.
Contains resources on women in geography and geographic studies of women in society, including current research.

589   Council of Planning Librarians. *The Women in American Society: A Selected Bibliography.* Exchange Bibliographies, nos. 810–811. 1974. Reprint. Monticello, Ill.: Council of Planning Librarians, 1975. 99 p., pb.
Includes short unannotated lists of general references, selected periodicals, organizations, and women college presidents, plus the test of the act establishing the Women's Bureau in 1920. Contains a chronological listing of Women's Bureau publications (1918–1971), a section of autobiography and biography divided by white women and black women, and a section of general interest books on women.

590   Dasgupta, Kalpana. *Women on the Indian Scene: An Annotated Bibliography.* New Delhi: Abhinau, 1976. 389 p.
Over eight hundred annotated citations of English-language sources on Indian women. Materials and topics include research trends, general studies, social problems, economics, politics, legal studies, education, art and culture, and biographies. Also included are lists of libraries, periodicals, anthologies, theses, and legislation.

591   Davis, Audrey B. *Bibliography on Women: With Special Emphasis on Their Roles in Science and Society.* New York: Science History Publications, 1974. 50 p., pb.
An unannotated selection of books and articles from the Library of Congress catalog, in simple alphabetical order. Some foreign language; topics include history, science, biography, and medicine.

592   Davis, Lenwood G. *The Black Woman in American Society: A Selected Annotated Bibliography.* 1974. Reprint. Boston: G. K. Hall, 1975. 145 p.
A compilation of 305 annotated books and 256 annotated articles. Contains autobiography, biography, fiction, and sociological analyses. Also general reference works, journals, pamphlets, documents. Lists black women in government and journalism, and national organizations of black women. Thorough.

593   Dubow, Rhona. *The Status of Women in South Africa: A Select Bibliography.* Cape Town: University of Cape Town School of Librarianship, 1965. 55 p., pb.
Though somewhat out of date, this annotated bibliography is particularly useful in locating material in South African journals and legal information in

statutes and legislation (with the exception of African "tribal" law). Two hundred citations.

594 Feminist Theory Collective. *American Women: Our Lives and Labor: An Annotated Bibliography on Women and Work in the United States, 1900–1975.* Eugene, Ore.: Feminist Theory Collective, 1976. 36 p., pb.
Designed as a study guide: a general section is followed by a chronological division of the sources. The authors emphasize readability, include books and articles concerning Third World women, treat housework as work, and stress descriptive over theoretical material. This is an extensively annotated and very useful pamphlet; it has many photographs.

595 Harrison, Cynthia Ellen. *Women's Movement Media: A Source Guide.* New York: R. R. Bowker, 1975. 269 p., pb.
A list of women's groups and publications, including governmental agencies. Indexed by geographic area, title of media, group name, and subject of groups. Particularly useful in locating ephemeral material and community organizations. Includes nonprint material such as films, speakers, records, radio shows. The inclusion of bookstores and feminist products (jewelry, posters) indicates its comprehensive nature.

596 Hughes, Marija Matich. *The Sexual Barrier: Legal and Economic Aspects of Employment.* San Francisco: M. M. Hughes, 1970. 35 p., pb.
Unannotated bibliography of books and articles on "the laws and conditions governing the employment of women" (preface). Divided by topic: legal aspects, discrimination, difference in pay, professional opportunities, and a general category. Includes government publications.

597 Jacobs, Sue-Ellen. *Women in Perspective: A Guide for Cross-Cultural Studies.* Urbana: University of Illinois Press, 1974. 236 p., pb.
A selected, primarily anthropological, bibliography of books, articles, periodicals on women. Divided into culture areas of Africa, Middle East, Asia, Europe, Oceania, South America, and North America (with subdivisions by country); subject areas include primate studies, psychological studies, sexuality, socialization, family/marriage, economics, education, history, literature, and religion. Includes most older (pre–1965) sources, with less emphasis on works since 1965. Not annotated. Indexed by author. Valuable.

598 Kelly, Joan. *Bibliography in the History of European Women.* 4th rev. ed. Bronxville, N.Y.: Sarah Lawrence College, Women's Studies Program, 1976. 132 p., pb.
These bibliographies are unannotated, arranged both chronologically and by subject, and include the topics of historiography, sexuality, law, family, work, education, biography and autobiography, literature, revolutionary thought

and practice. As organized book and article lists, these are useful in alerting users to the wealth of sources that deal in some way with women's experience.

599 Knaster, Meri. "Women in Latin America: The State of Research, 1975." *Latin American Research Review* 11, no. 1 (1976): 3–74.
A review essay in supplement to the G. K. Hall bibliography (no. 600), presenting themes and trends in research, as well as listing research in progress and an unannotated bibliography of recent works, including conference papers not listed in the longer bibliography.

600 Knaster, Meri. *Women in Spanish America: An Annotated Bibliography from Pre-Conquest to Contemporary Times.* Boston: G. K. Hall, 1977. 631 p.
A compilation of 2,534 annotated articles, books, unpublished Master's theses and Ph.D. dissertations, periodicals, and bibliographies on women in Middle America, South America, and the Spanish-speaking Caribbean published through 1974. Contains author and subject index. Annotations are informative. Monumental work. Extremely useful.

601 Kratochvil, Laura, and Shauna Shaw. *African Women: A Select Bibliography.* Cambridge: Cambridge University, African Studies Centre, 1974. Unpaged, pb.
A collection of 1,210 unannotated entries of books and articles on African women. Divided by subjects: the arts, general development studies, economics, elites, family, legal position, sexual relations, urban studies, ornamentation, politics, women's organizations, youth, religion, and ritual. Also indexed by region and author. Thorough; extremely useful.

602 Krichmar, Albert, et al. *The Women's Rights Movement in the United States 1848–1970: A Bibliography and Sourcebook.* Metuchen, N.J.: Scarecrow Press, 1972. 436 p.
A partially annotated listing on legal, political, and economic status, education, religion; includes biographies, manuscripts, and serials, as well as serial, manuscript, author, and subject indexes. The over five thousand sources also include lectures and newspaper articles, books, journals, and similar resources.

603 Leonard, Eugenie Andruss; Sophie Hutchinson Drinker; and Miriam Young Holden. *The American Woman in Colonial and Revolutionary Times, 1585–1800: A Syllabus with Bibliography.* Philadelphia: University of Pennsylvania Press, 1962. 169 p.
The syllabus is divided into ten subject areas, including the English and European backgrounds of women immigrants, heroic and patriotic activities, education, productive life, and charitable activities. The bibliography has over one thousand citations. Now outdated, though may be useful in conjunction with other sources.

604 Lerner, Gerda. *Bibliography in the History of American Women*. 2d rev. ed. Bronxville, N.Y.: Sarah Lawrence College, Women's Studies Program, 1975. 56 p., pb.
See Kelly, Joan, no. 598.

605 Martin, Diana. *Women in Chinese Society*. Annotated Bibliography no. 28. Oxford: Commonwealth Bureau of Agricultural Economics, 1974. 20 p., pb.
This bibliography contains 172 articles, books, and theses, primarily on Chinese and English material published since 1949. It is sporadically annotated, indexed by subject, and lists source for each citation.

606 McKee, Kathleen Burke. *Women's Studies: A Guide to Reference Sources*. University of Connecticut Library, Storrs, Bibliography Series, no. 6. Storrs: University of Connecticut, 1977. 112 p., pb.
An annotated guide to 364 reference sources on women. Includes guides, catalogs, library collections, directories, statistics, indexes, abstracts, and bibliographies. Reference in anthropology, art and architecture, business and economics, education, employment, films, geography, health, history, humanities, law, literature, philosophy, political science, psychology, population, sociology, religion, and women's studies are presented. Indexed by author, title, and subject.

607 Murray, Jocelyn. *A Preliminary Bibliography: Women in Africa*. Los Angeles: University of California, Graduate Women in History, 1974. 43 p., pb.
Approximately 860 unannotated citations on African women. Contains mostly articles. Divided by subject and country. Extremely useful and thorough.

608 *News and Reviews*, no. 8 (December 1975). "Recent Books on Indian Women."
Includes reviews of recent publications and annotated lists of sources on women in India.

609 Nicolas, Suzanne. *Bibliography on Women Workers (1861–1965)*. Geneva: International Labour Office, 1970. 252 p., pb.
Unannotated bibliography of over 1,700 international sources in English, French, German, Spanish, Russian, Hebrew, Italian, other languages. Organized chronologically within topics: education, employment, equal pay, occupations, conditions, legislation, married women and maternity protection, older workers, part-time workers, women's and professional organizations. Indexed by personal author, corporate author, subject, and geographic area. Includes books, articles, government publications. Particularly useful for international sources.

610   Parker, William. *Homosexuality: A Selective Bibliography of Over 3,000 Items.* Metuchen, N.J.: Scarecrow Press, 1971. 323 p.
An annotated bibliography of academic and popular books, articles (newspaper, journal, magazine), pamphlets and documents, court cases, theses and dissertations, literary works, and media productions before 1969. Contains both subject and author indexes.

611   Rosenberg, Marie, and Len Bergstrom. *Women and Society: A Critical Review of the Literature with a Selected Annotated Bibliography.* Beverly Hills: Sage, 1975. 354 p.
A collection of 3,503 books, articles, and periodicals. Also biographical dictionaries, directory of women's organizations, newspapers, and women's collections in libraries. Subject divisions are sociology, political science, history, philosophy, medicine, literature, psychology, economics, and anthropology. Largest number of references are in political science, history, and sociology sections. Most citations are briefly annotated. Extremely valuable.

612   Rowbotham, Sheila. *Women's Liberation and Revolution: A Bibliography.* 1972. Reprint. London: Falling Wall Press, 1973. 24 p., pb.
"This bibliography lists books, pamphlets, and articles which explore the relationship between feminism and revolutionary politics" (preface). It is a general introduction, based on what Rowbotham read for *Women, Resistance, and Revolution* (no. 206). Topics: general feminist history, women and puritan revolution, eighteenth century and the French Revolution, early radical and socialist movements, Marx and Engels, the family (nineteenth century), socialist and anarchist movements, Britain in early twentieth century, Russian revolution, China, imperialism, gay liberation, black women's liberation, wage work and trade unions, birth control, spiritualism. Annotated.

613   Soltow, Martha Jane, and Mary K. Wery. *American Women and the Labor Movement, 1825–1975: An Annotated Bibliography.* Metuchen, N.J.: Scarecrow Press, 1976. 247 p.
Seven hundred sources, organized by topic: employment (includes wartime problems), trade unions (problems, attitudes toward women, leadership), working conditions, strikes, legislation, worker education, labor leaders, support work (National Women's Trade Union League, Coalition of Labor Union Women). Includes an appendix of archival sources and indexes on cross-references, subjects, and authors. Includes books, articles, autobiographies. Substantial annotations. Includes Women's Bureau materials and many sources from labor newspapers (*Union WAGE, Life and Labor,* union publications). Excellent.

614   Strunin, Marion Harris. *American Women: A Research Guide to U.S. Government Sources.* Los Angeles: University of California, School of Library Service, February 1974. 74 p., pb.

A comprehensive guide that includes how to find and obtain specific publications, a survey of major federal publications that have "potentially useful information," and examples of current monographic material. Extremely useful—the method and guidelines presented are easily extended to more current material as well.

615 United Nations Secretariat. *Status of Women: A Selected Bibliography.* ST/LIB/SER.B./20. New York: United Nations, 1975. 121 p., pb.
Includes publications of the last ten years, mainly from the collection in the Dag Hammarskjöld Library, and other relevant material. Divided by topic (society, political participation, employment, professions, education, legal status, family, and population) and then by area (Europe, North America, Africa, Asia, Latin America, USSR, Oceania). Lists much useful material, including all relevant U.N. publications, and much non-Western material. Lists publications published in English, French, Spanish, Arabic, and many other languages.

616 U.S. Department of Health, Education and Welfare. Office of Education. Bureau of Occupational and Adult Education. *Women in Non-Traditional Occupations—A Bibliography.* Washington, D.C., 1976. 189 p., pb.
Annotated bibliography of magazine and journal articles, books, dissertations, pamphlets, brochures, and government documents published between January 1970 and June 1976. Sections on general information about women in the work force, vocational jobs, and professional occupations. Indexed by author, title, and subject/occupation and includes list of sources and resources for additional material.

617 Walstedt, Joyce. *The Psychology of Women: A Partially Annotated Bibliography.* Pittsburgh: International Standard Book, 1972. 76 p., pb.
Approximately six hundred citations—primarily articles, with some books and bibliographies on women's psychology. Many references are annotated. Divided by subject: infancy and childhood, adolescence, young adulthood, middle and old age; cross-cultural, general source materials, primate studies, minority group studies, psychoanalytic theories, sexuality, and physiology. Thorough.

618 Weinberg, Martin S., and Alan P. Bell. *Homosexuality: An Annotated Bibliography.* New York: Harper and Row, 1972. 550 p.
Extensive and scholarly annotations of 1,265 articles, books, bibliographies, and dissertations. Emphasis on academic rather than popular publications. Combines psychological, psychiatric, and sociological literature. Etiology, assessments, treatment are emphasized in psychology and psychiatric sections. Homosexual community and history, together with societal attitudes and legal considerations of homosexuals, are highlighted in sociological literature. Citations from 1940 to 1968. Both subject and author indexes. Valuable resource.

619   Westervelt, Esther Manning, and Deborah A. Fixter. *Women's Higher and Continuing Education: An Annotated Bibliography with Selected References on Related Aspects of Women's Lives.* New York: College Entrance Examination Board, 1971. 67 p., pb.
Extensive notes on books and articles, particularly pertaining to women and education (very broadly defined). Some general history.

620   Wheeler, Helen. *Womanhood Media: Current Resources about Women.* Metuchen, N.J.: Scarecrow Press, 1972. 335 p.
This resource book has several disparate sections; the first, called an "awareness inventory," is a quiz on feminist issues and history. The rest of the book is devoted to a more conventional guide, with information on the use of reference sources, an annotated "basic book collection," a list of movement periodicals and special issues of other journals on women, a guide to audio-visual resources, and a directory to other resources. This is a very personal collection, with an arrogant tone to it; the audio-visual guide is by far the most useful section.

621   Wheeler, Helen Rippier. *Womanhood Media Supplement: Additional Current Resources about Women.* Metuchen, N.J.: Scarecrow Press, 1975. 482 p.
To be used in conjunction with Wheeler's 1972 volume (no. 620). Includes sections on basic books, non-book resources (pamphlets, periodicals, and audio-visual material), and a directory to other sources (women's centers, commissions, speakers, and consultants). Wheeler's notes include suitability for high school use and availability in Spanish. Some annotations are informative, others almost useless. Due to the personal nature of selection, this has limited usefulness as a guide to what is available. Again, the audio-visual list is the most useful. Only the basic books are indexed.

622   Williams, Ora. *American Black Women in the Arts and Sciences: A Bibliographical Survey.* Metuchen, N.J.: Scarecrow Press, 1973. 135 p.
Approximately one thousand unannotated citations by and/or about black women. References are primarily in literature (novels, poetry, anthologies, biographies), although some are from education, history, sociology, and political science.

623   *Women in the Working Class.* Radical America Pamphlet. Boston: New England Free Press, 1973. 36 p., pb.
A collection of reviews of mainly historical books dealing with working women. The reviews are thorough and from a radical political perspective.

624   Women's Educational Equity Communications Network. *Resources in Women's Educational Equity, Volume 1.* Washington, D.C.: U.S. Department of Health, Education and Welfare, 1977. 298 p., pb.

Articles, dissertations, and books (published in 1976) on topics of women and education, health, careers, sex differences, "life style," and legal issues. Scholarly, lengthy abstracts of each citation are provided. References for this compilation are ERIC ABI/INFORM, *Dissertation Abstracts International, Agricola, Medlars, Psychological Abstracts, Sociological Abstracts,* and National Technical Information Service. Detailed subject and author indexes. Valuable resource.

625 Women's Studies Department and Women's History Library. *Bibliographies on Women: Indexed by Topic.* Berkeley: Women's History Research Center, 1973. 8 p., pb.
A short but useful listing of bibliographies, including books with good bibliographies.

626 Woodsworth, Anne, comp. *Women: A Guide to Bibliographic Sources.* Toronto: University of Toronto, Library, 1974. 26 p., pb.
Evaluative annotations of bibliographic material available at their library. Useful. Includes bibliographies, biographical sources, course syllabi, dictionaries and lexicons, and some journals.

Journals

627 *Archives of Sexual Behavior: An Interdisciplinary Journal of Research.*
A bimonthly scholarly journal devoted to the study of human and relevant nonhuman sexual behavior. Material from all disciplines. Book reviews also included.

628 *Canadian Newsletter of Research on Women.*
Focuses on ongoing Canadian research, although includes international, especially Australian, material. May 1977 issue includes a supplement on archival materials on Canadian women. Tries *not* to have U.S. material to avoid duplication. Book reviews, especially of Canadian material; positions for women in Canadian universities; bibliographies, recent publications, annotated; Canadian theses; periodicals and other resources; review essays; courses being taught (and outlines); conference announcements.

629 *Comment: On Research about Wo/men.*
A quarterly publication that presents abstracts of recent events of interest to women in educational institutions and the latest research in social sciences and literature. Some issues focus on a theme, for example, women and work. Informative.

630 *Feminist Studies.*
Quarterly journal, Interdisciplinary and scholarly articles. Predominantly history. Useful.

631   *Frontiers: A Journal of Women Studies.*
Provides interdisciplinary scholarly articles published in conjunction with Women's Studies Department, University of Colorado.

632   *Journal of Homosexuality.*
A quarterly journal begun in Fall 1974. Presents empirical research and analysis of lesbianism, male homosexuality, gender identity, and "alternative lifestyles" from anthropology, sociology, psychology, medicine, and law. Also provides editorials and book reviews. Volume one, number one, contains a review of the literature on female homosexuality by B. Reiss.

633   *Journal of Reprints of Documents Affecting Women.*
Documents of historical importance affecting women—laws, court decisions. Started July 1976—first two years will be devoted to reprinting documents of the past decade, as well as the most recent material issued. Includes an abstract with each official copy of the document. Contains subject index (subject areas, organizations, individuals, court cases, laws) and annual cumulative index. Well done.

634   *Journal of Sex Research.*
A scholarly journal devoted to study of sexuality, specifically those factors influencing sexual behavior. Published quarterly. Much valuable theory and empirical research.

635   *Media Report to Women: What Women Are Doing and Thinking about the Communications Media.*
A monthly newsletter that provides information about women in television, radio, newspapers. Lists new publications (magazines, newsletters), jobs, and organizations.

636   *Peer Perspectives.*
A newsletter published by the Project on Equal Education Rights, National Organization for Women, specifically to "monitor enforcement progress under federal law forbidding sex discrimination in education" (Title IX). Focuses on latest developments, especially legal issues, in education pertinent to women.

637   *Psychology of Women Quarterly.*
First issue in Fall 1976, this scholarly journal presents current research and theory on psychobiological factors, behavior studies, role development, career choice and training, education, discrimination, therapeutic processes, and sexuality of women. Abstracts of articles and book reviews are provided. Summer 1977 issue contains a review of films.

638   *Quest: A Feminist Quarterly.*
Articles structured by theme of each issue (e.g., "women, fame, and power").

Deals with contemporary topics pertinent to women (e.g., work, business, therapy).

639   *Sex Roles: A Journal of Research.*
An interdisciplinary scholarly journal providing theoretical and empirical articles on "sex role socialization and change in children and adults." Journal divided into sections: research articles, theoretical articles, and book reviews. Publishes much recent research. Extremely valuable.

640   *Signs: Journal of Women in Culture and Society.*
An excellent scholarly journal that focuses on the social sciences and humanities. Includes regular contributions in the fields of history, anthropology, literary criticism, political science, sociology, psychology, economics, philosophy. Book reviews, archives (letters and other previously unpublished material), reports of ongoing research, and review essays in various disciplines. Special issues on China, religion, development, supplement on women in the workplace. Extremely wide ranging and informative. U.S. and international notes on research, conferences, and other information.

641   *University of Michigan Papers in Women's Studies.*
Published by students, faculty, and community of University of Michigan. Includes reviews, comments, articles, bibliographies, monographs, and excerpts of dissertations from most disciplines. Useful material.

642   *Women: A Journal of Liberation.*
A collectively produced journal which is comprised primarily of contributions on particular themes. Includes graphics and poetry as well as stories and articles, presenting personal experience in a political context. Issues have included women as workers, women in history, international women, androgyny, cost of living, children, aging.

643   *Women Studies Abstracts.*
A quarterly publication that provides abstracts of articles on the topics of women and education, socialization, sex roles and sex characteristics, sexuality, family, government, religion, mental and physical health, history, literature and art, media, interpersonal relations, and liberation movement. Also three to four book reviews, review essays, and articles on women per issue. Abstracts, reviews, and articles indexed by author and subject. Lists new books, and books on women that are reviewed in other journals (usually twenty to thirty per issue). Abstracts, reviews, and articles are succinct and scholarly. A valuable resource.

644   *Women's Studies: An Interdisciplinary Journal.*
Scholarly articles from literature, history, law, political science, economics, anthropology, and sociology. Useful.

645 *Women's Studies Newsletter.*
Published quarterly. Contains articles on teaching and new developments in women's studies. Includes bibliographies, new books, job advertisements, and new publications on women. For 1977–78 incorporates the official newsletter of the National Women's Studies Association.

Other Resources

646 Betancourt, Jeanne. *Women in Focus.* Dayton: Pflaum, 1974. 186 p., pb.
A guide to films that deal with women in nonsexist ways, including many on sexuality and sex education. Includes suggested accompanying readings, companion films, and long, readable, informative reviews, with information on the filmmaker. International and multicultural also. Indexed by title, filmmaker, theme.

647 Boulding, Elise; Shirley A. Nuss; Dorothy Lee Carson; and Michael A. Greenstein. *Handbook of International Data on Women.* New York: John Wiley and Sons, Halstead Press; and Beverly Hills: Sage, 1976. 468 p.
This reference work presents computer-coded information on women's economic activities (including industries in which women participate, occupations, and status); literacy and education; immigration; marital status; life, death, and reproduction; and political and civic participation. The information is from U.N. sources. A good resource for statistical information.

648 Dawson, Bonnie. *Women's Films in Print.* San Francisco: Bootlegger Press, 1975. 165 p., pb.
Organized alphabetically by filmmaker (370); includes 800 films, descriptive notes, although with little suggestion as to audience, and bibliography of further information. Films are not limited to subject of women. Indexed by title, subject.

649 *Female Studies.* Old Westbury, N.Y.: Feminist Press.
Ten volumes (1971[?] through 1976) on women's studies courses in the social sciences, languages, and literature. Volumes variously provide methods for teaching women's studies courses, descriptions and syllabi of courses already taught, bibliographies for areas of study, students' work, comments by professors on teaching, and papers on topics relevant to course work. Invaluable tool.

650 *International Directory of Women's Development Organizations.* Edited by Franziska P. Hoxten. Washington, D.C.: Agency for International Development, 1977. 311 p., pb.
This directory lists 289 local and national women's organizations by country. Information provided about the organizations includes chapters, membership,

publications, functions, activities, officers, and locations. "Master chart" lists organizations by functions and areas.

651   James, Edward T.; Janet Wilson James; and Paul S. Boyer, eds. *Notable American Women 1607–1950: A Biographical Dictionary.* Cambridge: Mass.: Harvard University Press, Belknap Press, 1971. 3 v., pb.
A fascinating guide to women in American history—arranged alphabetically, with approximately a page of biography on each of the 1,337 women included. Sources of information on each individual are appended to each biography. Individuals are listed in occupational index at end of book. Important source.

652 Kowalski, Rosemary Ribich. *Women and Film: A Bibliography.* Metuchen, N.J.: Scarecrow Press, 1976. 278 p.
An excellent annotated guide to all aspects of women and films, such as performers, filmmakers, and images of women. Kowalski has included reference works, books, articles, and catalogs, as well as lists of women columnists and critics. This is not a catalog of films with ordering information. Includes subject index; over 2,300 listings.

653   Smith, Sharon. *Women Who Make Movies.* New York: Hopkinson and Blake, 1975. 307 p., pb.
Information on women filmmakers and distribution of their films both in the U.S. and, more briefly, internationally. Organized by filmmaker, material is included on the subject matter of films and the history of women filmmakers in the U.S.

654 Women's History Research Center. *Films By and/or About Women, 1972: Directory of Filmmakers, Films, and Distributors, Internationally, Past and Present.* Berkeley: Women's History Research Center, 1972. 72 p., pb.
Topical organization, annotated, with ordering information; comprehensive rather than selective listings.

Author Index

Subject Index

Achievement, 170, 359, 364, 365, 382, 389, 390, 553

Adolescence, 112, 390, 401, 406, 414, 449, 518, 523, 617

Africa, 1, 2, 6, 11, 15, 19, 23, 24, 25, 35, 36, 37, 38, 39, 40, 41, 42, 43, 44, 46, 47, 48, 49, 51, 52, 53, 77, 97, 143, 145, 171, 206, 272, 278, 281, 282, 287, 479, 524, 571, 597, 601, 607, 615

Aging, 122, 124, 235, 291, 367, 376, 433, 442, 451, 496, 504, 582, 617, 642

Agricultural and horticultural societies, 3, 9, 14, 18, 42, 108, 498

Androgyny, 359, 360, 366, 373, 390, 434, 509, 642

Animal studies, 360, 364, 371, 392, 396, 400, 627

Archaeology, 16, 68

Asia, 10, 15, 19, 36, 54, 58, 97, 179, 192, 206, 276, 278, 280, 291, 292, 295, 388, 433, 534, 560, 597, 615

Associations and organizations, 23, 29, 48, 49, 52, 53, 60, 63, 66, 67, 75, 86, 87, 92, 96, 103, 111, 195, 204, 212, 221, 259, 262, 263, 264, 265, 267, 268, 272, 275, 281, 283, 284, 286, 287, 328, 333, 336, 354, 436, 464, 476, 481, 498, 564, 567, 584, 589, 595, 601, 609, 611, 613, 645, 650

Attitudes toward women, 144, 187, 196, 201, 213, 214, 243, 253, 274, 278, 297, 302, 305, 310, 320, 329, 351, 368, 434, 446, 510, 539, 542, 544, 549, 551, 613

Australia, 27, 107, 109, 111, 179, 411, 435, 628

Autobiography and biography, 12, 20, 24, 37, 45, 51, 57, 69, 74, 79, 88, 99, 100, 105, 119, 154, 158, 159, 167, 169, 189, 207, 215, 221, 222, 225, 234, 237, 239, 245, 247, 250, 251, 258, 260, 263, 267, 275, 277, 279, 280, 288, 289, 293, 297, 300, 308, 309, 332, 340, 345, 349, 352, 370, 445, 451, 458, 467, 487, 540, 545, 559, 583, 586, 589, 590, 591, 592, 598, 602, 613, 651

Black women, 117, 133, 174, 190, 207, 215, 224, 234, 236, 238, 259, 282, 341, 343, 354, 358, 364, 367, 431, 438, 441, 444, 449, 466, 477, 487, 494, 495, 502, 506, 532, 554, 565, 570, 571, 577, 578, 586, 589, 592, 612, 622

Canada, 1, 15, 19, 98, 105, 283, 289, 293, 355, 460, 498, 628

Capitalism, 27, 76, 79, 313, 460, 479, 480, 484, 570, 575

Caribbean, 61, 62, 63, 64, 65, 66, 67, 76, 78, 297, 436, 600

Central America, 1, 11, 15, 28, 68, 70, 71, 72, 73, 76, 77, 78, 79, 121, 143, 145, 146, 200, 220, 282, 288, 290, 294, 365, 367, 388, 479, 524, 534, 599, 600, 615

Chicanas, 220, 358, 457, 482, 487, 556, 570, 575, 585, 586

Childcare, 9, 13, 16, 17, 22, 34, 40, 41, 52, 66, 95, 124, 132, 179, 180, 182, 183, 185, 188, 191, 211, 298, 324, 350, 371, 386, 398, 415, 437, 465, 493, 495, 568, 573

Childhood, 279, 365, 369, 378, 379, 390, 396, 401, 402, 406, 414, 452, 505, 523, 527, 537, 601, 617

China, 19, 23, 28, 36, 57, 59, 60, 121, 196, 206, 279, 280, 284, 285, 286, 291, 298, 299, 300, 301, 303, 304, 374, 388, 391, 434, 448, 524, 536, 538, 571, 605, 612, 640

Christianity, 43, 63, 67, 73, 301, 308, 309, 311, 428, 437, 471, 477, 558

Civil War (U.S.), 223, 238, 244

Guide to Social Science Resources in Women's Studies was
compiled by Elizabeth H. Oakes and Kathleen E. Sheldon. For
the publisher: copyediting by Paulette Wamego, proofing by Jean Holzinger
and Paul Behrens, typography by Shelly Lowenkopf.
Cover design and execution by Graphics Two, Los Angeles;
composition in Goudy Old Style by McAdams Type, Santa Barbara.
Offset printing and bindery work by
Edwards Brothers, Inc., Ann Arbor, Mich.